Father to the Immigrants

The Servant of God
BISHOP JOHN BAPTIST SCALABRINI
[1839—1905]
Founder of The Missionaries of St. Charles

Father to the Immigrants

The Servant of God

JOHN BAPTIST SCALABRINI
Bishop of Piacenza

BY

ICILIO FELICI

TRANSLATED BY CAROL DELLA CHIESA

P. J. KENEDY & SONS
NEW YORK

Nihil Obstat: Very Reverend Armand Barrette, Censor Librorum
Imprimatur: John J. Wright, D.D., Bishop of Worcester

Worcester, Massachusetts
August 31, 1955

"It is my belief that the religious and moral greatness of the future of the Italian immigrants is bound to blend with the political and material greatness of the United States. The result will abound in blessings from God and great achievements for civilization. It will reveal the secrets of a new era to the twentieth century."

(THE SERVANT OF GOD J. B. SCALABRINI)

Contents

Preface

A CHORUS of fervent and continuous prayer rises from the many houses, missions, parishes and schools of the Missionaries of St. Charles, begging God for the favor of having their founder, Giovanni Battista Scalabrini, raised to the honors of the altar. This Servant of God attained a glorious and gigantic stature in the annals of the Church and of his country. In this biography the author, Icilio Felici, depicts and describes, with painstaking accuracy and sincere devotion, the founder of the Pious Society of the Missionaries of St. Charles, especially in his role as bishop and missionary.

Bishop Scalabrini, reacting with holy indifference to human acclaim, received many honors, and his fame, following the trail of his good works, quickly spread beyond the confines of Piacenza and Italy. His activity, so genial and prodigious, drew its inspiration from an ardent flame nurtured by prayer —the charity of Christ impelled him (II Cor. 5:14). Humble and pious from early youth, a most exemplary priest and a zealous bishop at the early age of thirty-six, he was deeply conscious of the presence of God and centered his life in the Holy Eucharist. Most of his decisions were preceded by a visit to the most Blessed Sacrament and those of particular importance were deferred until after the celebration of Holy Mass. Gentle of character and firm of will, he was courageous in his decisions and his work. He was unrelenting in defending religion and protecting the weak and oppressed, and he was always *"ad omne opus bonum paratus"* with the same self-sacrificing generosity for social duties recommended by

1

St. Paul (Tit. 3:1). In times of epidemic he risked contagion by attending the sick and dying, and in times of famine he fed the hungry, even at the cost of converting his most cherished possessions and sacred objects into the price of food. Thousands upon thousands of poor received nourishment and clothing from his hands. He sought them out, and with a sympathetic understanding of their needs, consoled and helped them.

No human need or misery escaped his pastoral vigilance. He visited the sick, paying particular attention and making special efforts in behalf of those who might not have been inclined to respond to the spiritual ministry of the local priest. He opened recreational centers, day nurseries and training schools, and an institute for the deaf and dumb. He promoted social-economic action, a good Catholic press, and introduced Catholic action in every parish at a time when it was practically unknown in the form which is so familiar in our day. He showed a particularly watchful and affectionate concern for young men who aspired to the priesthood. He gave them personal direction, always with a view to providing the sanctuary with elect souls and the people with holy and zealous pastors after the Heart of Jesus Christ. In faithful pursuance of one of his rules—never to waste a moment of time—despite the variety and multiplicity of his apostolic activities, he was able to devote hours to the study of sacred sciences.

Bishop Scalabrini was, above all, a shepherd of souls. He lived for his clergy and for the faithful of his diocese.

He so distinguished himself in his intensive and extensive program of catechetical instruction that the Sovereign Pontiff, Pius IX, hailed him as "Apostle of the Catechism." It seemed as if St. Charles Borromeo lived once again in him. He introduced a program of catechetical instruction in every parish. He revised the text of the diocesan catechism and trained large numbers of lay catechists. In 1889 he wrote a golden page in the history of the teaching of Catechism in

Italy by sponsoring a national catechetical congress in his episcopal city. The congress was truly successful, not only because of the great numbers of participating cardinals, bishops and priests, but because of its enduring salutary influence upon the teaching of Catechism throughout Italy.

His pastoral letters, conference and sermons reached and influenced even those outside the fold. He founded the review, *Divus Thomas*, not for the sake of being a patron, but for the purpose of popularizing the principles of perennial philosophy and of stimulating sound Catholic theological thought. His love for the house of the Lord impelled him to find the means to restore the historic Cathedral of Piacenza, a task most difficult in those times, especially for one who had assumed the daily responsibility of carrying on his good works of charity and social assistance.

He was always a pioneer and, at times, even a forerunner, as, for example, in his efforts to promote the conciliation of the Church and State in Italy. In the face of sharp divergencies of opinions the unification of Italy had then been accomplished and anticlericals, capitalizing on the divergencies, strove to repress the Church's influence upon social life and to exile her from educational and charitable institutions. It was almost inevitable that a person who was so prominent, who aroused such enthusiasm and produced such great things should become the target of many attacks. He suffered much but never relented. His position was not inspired by any liberal tendency, as some might have been inclined to think, but by a sincere love for Church and country.

In the problem of emigration, Bishop Scalabrini was a true pioneer in Italy. He awakened the authorities and the entire nation to the needs of the emigrant. These needs became the subject of lively and effective discussion in the public press, in the parliament, and in every city. The emigrants required the assistance of priests distinguished as shepherds of souls and as guardians of the social and economic well-being of their charges. He made public appeals for priests who would volunteer to accompany the emigrants. Zealous priests responded to his call, and he organized them into the Pia Societá dei Missionari de San Carlo. Our Servant of God considered this project as a normal duty of his sacred ministry. A pastoral visitation of his diocese disclosed that 28,000 of his flock had emigrated and he was concerned about their spiritual and economic welfare. There was reason for such concern for, sad to say, the emigrants in those days were often ignored and exploited.

Such work of our bishop was eminently providential and inspired, and the author of this book describes its development. As in all great undertakings, difficulties ensued and the Holy See intervened to provide an added impetus to his program.

It was in the period following World War I that the Holy See, especially through the work of Cardinal Gaetano De Lai, then secretary of the Sacred Consistorial Congregation, undertook to reappraise the foundational strength of the Pia Societá, to determine its ability to fulfill its purposes, and to promote, within the measure of possibility, its greater expansion.

It was then my pleasant duty and privilege to come into personal contact with almost every spiritual son of the eminent apostle of emigration. I was named apostolic visitor of the Missionaries of St. Charles outside Italy, and visited those of North America in the summer of 1924, and two years later those in Brazil. I saw them personally, visiting the fields of their apostolate. In the various cities of the New World, in the large industrial and commercial centers, as well as in the small agricultural villages, wherever the emigrant found a home and work, the missionaries erected the houses of God. I visited churches for the Italians in New York, Chicago, Boston, Buffalo, Syracuse, Utica, New Haven, Kansas City, St. Louis, and Cincinnati. In Brazil, I visited those of Rio de

Janeiro, São Paulo, Paraná, Rio Grande do Sul, and others. I called at the villages of Santa Felicitade, Monte Veneto, Dois Lageados, and stations along the edge of the Brazilian forest, on the high woody plains, and along the banks of rivers rich in tropical vegetation. In these outposts, which at times were accessible only with difficulty by boat or on horseback, the good missionaries developed churches, schools, clinics, and recreational centers, and thus surrounded the emigrant with a fitting spiritual atmosphere so that his work —sustained by faith in God and nourished by love of neighbor—might be a safe means of preserving Christian civilization.

As a result of these visits I was able to make glowing reports of the beneficent, understanding, and fruitful work of the Missionaries of St. Charles. They measured up to the highest ideals of Bishop Scalabrini—ideals which he seemed to have infused into his spiritual sons. It was the desire and plan of the Holy See to effect a stronger union among the missionaries, to systematize their multiple activities, to augment their numbers by new recruits, and to extend their apostolate to other lands.

God has blessed "the small seed" which, with evangelical zeal, was planted in 1887 by the apostle of the emigrants. With paternal care Bishop Scalabrini watched over its first development, and God with His grace "has given the growth" to that seed and has rendered it fruitful (I Cor. 3:7). Under the careful and vigilant eye of the Church "it has grown up and become a tree, so that the birds of the air come and dwell in its branches" (Matt. 13:32). And truly the present 150 centers of the Missionaries of St. Charles offer to the emigrants what the branches of a tree offer to the birds of the air—comfort, assistance, protection in the salutary shade of Faith, and a bond of union with that great far-off family from which they came, Italy.

I am confident that this biography of Bishop Scalabrini

will be cordially welcomed by the public. It is my heartfelt wish that this book will have the widest possible circulation and the greatest number of readers. The facile and spirited pen of the author merits it; the valiant Missionaries of St. Charles who, with richness of zeal and sacrifice, bring the comforts of Faith and the smile of the fatherland to the emigrant, deserve it. But most of all, Bishop Scalabrini, whose pious death occurred just fifty years ago, is worthy of it. To read and to know his life is a pleasant tribute of praise, gratitude, and veneration to his hallowed memory. I consider it a high honor to present this book to the readers, as a token of my profound and humble homage to a worthy and saintly successor of the Apostles.

✠ A. G. Cicognani

Archbishop of Laodicea
Apostolic Delegate

Washington, D. C.
March 25, 1955

Foreword

I CONSIDER it a privilege as well as an honor to present to the public this new biography of the servant of God, John Baptist Scalabrini, candidate, as many of us fondly hope, to the honors of the altar.

I am sincerely glad of this opportunity, as I am so deep an admirer of the great Bishop of Piacenza. Through him and his work the Catholic episcopate was and is exalted. In him every bishop may find a model, the model of one who gave close attention to the exigencies of his times.

I have further cause for rejoicing as the present "protector" of that religious family known as the Pious Society of St. Charles Borromeo, the society founded by Bishop Scalabrini for the sole purpose of looking after the interests of Italian emigrants. It was through his efforts that the work of the Society won recognition, and its members today take pride in their illustrious founder and follow in his spirit and zeal.

Today the biographer of Bishop Scalabrini is guaranteed absolute accuracy by relying upon the basic facts given by Monsignor Francesco Gregori in *The Life and Works of a Great Bishop* (R. Berutti & Co., Turin, 1934). This biography is accurately and profusely documented. The author dedicated it to H. E. Carlo Raffaele Cardinal Rossi, still living at the time. His reason for the dedication, as he wrote, was "that with true intellectual devotion you protect and lead the greatest among the charitable achievements of Bishop Scalabrini. In restoring the pristine ideal of its great founder to its full integrity, you demonstrate how completely and you understand and appreciate his profound spirit."

7

The biographer of tomorrow will have at his disposal even more copious and authoritative sources when he is able to delve into the vast documentary evidence presented in the canonical cause now in process before the Sacred Congregation of Rites.

Meanwhile, the known facts in the life of Bishop Scalabrini have enabled the writer of the present work to draw a full and appealing portrait of the Servant of God. The author's intention is to give an accurate account, unencumbered by the weight of documentary evidence but exact in its informative data. His work offers fascinating reading and focuses attention upon his protagonist's loftiness of mind and magnificent achievements.

As the humble successor of Cardinal Rossi, I welcome a biography so well suited to its enlightening and edifying purpose. In the pages of this book Bishop Scalabrini truly returns among us to become part of our lives and of our times. The impact of his powerful personality and the great interest of the apostolic work he founded are definite guarantees of this.

While the saintly character of the Bishop of Piacenza is emerging in the canonical process now in progress, the historical figure of the man, far away in time though it may be, stands out ever more profound and more luminous. This is true even in the minutest details as he is seen against the turbulent background of the period in which he lived.

Cardinal Nasalli Rocca, of venerable memory, spoke truly of him when he said:

"The men who belong to history reveal all of their stupendous greatness when they are no longer our contemporaries. Then only do they divest themselves of that 'shadowy veil' that accompanies every 'real' figure."

And he adds, as though in an outburst of feeling:

"My Bishop! As the years roll by since your departure from this world, you have become greater in the history of Piacenza, of the Church, of Italy, and of that great young America!"

Bishop Scalabrini's living presence among us is assured through the grandiose work of his mind and energy which is continued on an ever-increasing scale. Historical events relative to the preoccupying problems of migration concur in deepening our appreciation of the timeliness of his actions and of his intuitive genius and wisdom as an organizer of institutes, societies and missions.

In a recent document of fundamental importance, the "Apostolic Constitution for the Care of Immigrants" (*Exul Familia*—August 1, 1952), the person of Bishop Scalabrini, pioneer and apostle, rises powerful and inspiring. The record of his work, of his "aliveness" among us, comes as if to encourage the efforts of the Church and of those who are dedicating themselves to the arduous mission of giving comfort and spiritual assistance to the tens of thousands who tread the road of the exile in search of work and of a better life, urged on by dire need or by an unkind fate.

In order to gain "good fruit" through the reading of these pages we should hold certain of Bishop Scalabrini's characteristics before our mind and eyes. These are as golden threads in the warp and the woof of this altogether splendid life. They will enable us better to comprehend the noble and at the same time complex personality of this bishop.

Bishop Scalabrini lived his almost threescore and ten years in the second half of the nineteenth century and in the dawn of the twentieth. For twenty-nine years he carried the heavy burden of one of the most important dioceses of Italy during difficult and harrowing days. The radius of his activities reached out beyond the oceans. I can touch upon them only lightly.

Vocation to the Missionary Life and Missionary Ideal. These were the dynamic forces latent in the whole of the bishop's life and work.

The following words were spoken by him at the end of his days:

"To win everyone to Christ! Behold this is the constant, the supreme aspiration of my soul!"

This desire of his soul for the conquest of souls for Christ was born of his priesthood. Hence he dreamed of pursuing his missionary vocation in the St. Calogero Institute for Foreign Missions. There is not the least doubt that he would have pursued the ideal burning in his heart had not his bishop said to him:

"I need you here. Your 'Indies' is 'Italy.' "

He made his renunciation, bowing in obedience to his superior, but his spirit remained unchanged.

As a bishop he was to say:

". . . the wooden cross of the missionary has been changed for me into the golden one I carry on my breast. This cross often leads me to burst forth in lamentations to my God, for having willed that I carry it rather than that other. But I cannot fail to say once again, 'May God's will be done in all things!' "

And yet, both as priest and as bishop, he lived and labored in conformity with his pristine idea.

"A bishop with the soul of a missionary," Cardinal Nasalli Rocca was to say of him.

Thus we can understand the reason for his turning to the emigrant world to crown his other admirable achievements. The Pious Missionary Institute of St. Charles, founded by him, is the projection into time of his sublime missionary ideal.

Apostolic Mission. Providence led him to this along unforeseen and admirable ways. The experiences of his ministry as a priest, as pastor in a difficult parish, as rector of a seminary, were one and all steps leading upward; they were also within the divine plant to mould within him the con-

science of a bishop, that is, of an apostle and a builder of
apostles.

Pius XII, our present pontiff, has defined him in these
words:

"An apostolic man, worthy of the Church and of his
country."

Bishop Scalabrini saw to it that his priests received a solid
foundation in piety and in doctrine, and promoted the reorganization of the Lombard Seminary in Rome. Later, in his
own diocese, he founded the ranks of the lay apostles of
Catholic Action, with a fine intuition of the needs of the new
times and the paths that Divine Providence had laid out for
him.

Pope Pius IX called him the "Apostle of the Catechism."
In fact he founded the periodical *The Catholic Catechist*,
organized catechistical congresses, and himself dictated the
text for a catechism intended for the youngest members of his
flock. He was always faithful to the suggestion made by Pius
IX, one which is of value to us also:

"Today, we pay too much attention to the second floor of
the house. Very little attention is paid the ground floor. The
Catechism is truly the foundation, whence any pastoral labor
of sermons must spring. Society is saved through good
catechisms."

Does this not touch directly upon the fundamental mission
of a bishop, the successor of the Apostles? Bishop Scalabrini
was deeply imbued with a sense of this apostolic duty. His
pastoral ministry was attuned to its meaning, particularly during those tedious and wearisome diocesan visits made in ever-
increasing rhythm to the end of his days. His voice, the voice
of an apostle of Christ, was heard not only in inspiring
talks and sermons, but also in numerous pastoral letters
rich in doctrine and in practical teaching. When he assumed
the tremendous and arduous task of caring for the Italian
emigrants he carried on with a spirit of dedication that in

later years spurred him to dare the hardships of two long journeys to North and South America. His outstanding achievement was the founding in Piacenza of the Apostolic Institute for the Emigrants, which he dedicated to Christopher Columbus.

Paternal Interest. We have here the general imprint of his personality and his pastoral life. A sense, deep and abiding, of a supernatural, fatherly responsibility that had grown within him during his years as a pastor rose in his episcopal years to the very heights, inspired and upheld by the exquisite feelings of a kind heart, open to any and all suffering humanity. Father to the poor, the worker, the sick, the deaf and dumb! His efforts knew no bounds. They took on heroic lines during the terrible days when cholera broke out in his parish and in the days when famine stalked his diocese of Piacenza. He was a kind and vigilant father to his seminarians, to his beloved priests, to his missionaries. For these he reserved particular attention, for him they represented those who were interpreting and fulfilling in an often heroic manner the profound and vast apostolic plans which were closest to his mind and heart.

Bishop Scalabrini has been called "Father to the Emigrants." This was not through mere empty sentimentality. His fatherly spirit drew strength from a supernatural understanding and from that charity that is the fruitful mother of miracles. The life of this bishop appears as though sown with the miracles wrought by charity. He himself had this to say to the Italian clergy when recalling their attention to the problem of emigration:

"Charity, true breath of God, knows no party. The Sacred Blood of Christ makes us brethren, joined together into one faith, and only one hope. It makes debtors of us all!"

The Cross and the Crucifix. Behold the sources of Bishop Scalabrini's fathomless spiritual energy! When Pius IX offered him a magnificent pectoral cross and chain at the beginning of his episcopate—a cross that he later sold to raise funds to feed the hungry during the Great Famine—he did not fail to remind him that "a bishop's cross is precious, but heavier by far . . ."

Bishop Scalabrini experienced to the full the truth of these words in a life of labor, struggle, and suffering. This was the secret of his personal sanctity and of his success in his apostolic enterprises.

Perhaps most interesting among the pages of this biography are those which hold him before us as a true fighter ("agonist" is the liturgical term) in his battle to uphold the integrity of the Faith, the liberty of the Church, the decorum of the episcopal dignity, and in his filial devotion to the Vicar of Christ on earth.

Neither the "libelists" of a certain Catholic sector, those of whom St. Paul speaks as the "false brethren," nor the venomous champions of Freemasonry with their campaign of insult and vituperation, could break or even weaken the rockbound soul of the fearless bishop. This bitter cup, however, although accepted courageously during his battles in defense of truth and justice, perhaps more than the hardships of his pastoral life, more than his illnesses and his penances, tended to shorten his life. True it is that they increased to the merit and the "good fruit" of his episcopal years "to fill up those things that are wanting of the suffering of Christ . . . for his Body, which is the Church" (Col. 1:24).

He who wishes to summarize the life and the works of Bishop Scalabrini may state without fear of contradiction that he splendidly fulfilled the words of St. Paul:

". . . take heed to yourselves and to the whole flock wherein the Holy Ghost hath placed you, bishops, to rule the Church of God which he hath purchased with his own Blood" (Acts 20:28).

The figure of Bishop Scalabrini rises dominant in his century. He was certainly a man of action. His activities were wide in scope and were beneficial far beyond the boundaries of his diocese and his native land. The popes of his time, Pius IX, Leo XIII, and Pius X, all were prodigal in their affectionate marks of regard for him.

Bishop Bonomelli, another outstanding shepherd, was his devoted friend. St. Frances Xavier Cabrini, who later was to become "Mother and Patroness to the Italian Emigrants," received advice and help from him. Cardinals, bishops, and civic authorities lent their aid and gave of their admiration. All these things place our bishop in the forefront of the ecclesiastical and civic history of his time.

"Enlightened and tireless worker," "Shepherd of the poor and the Unfortunates," "Patron of the Emigrants," these were and are sincere and enthusiastic judgments of him.

The following article written as a tribute to him on the occasion of his episcopal jubilee speaks for itself:

"A personality full of charm, a bishop kind of character, ardent in zeal, generous of soul, one with an intuitive sense of the material and moral needs of his flock; a man of God who uses the deep intuitions of his mind and the generous impulses of his heart, and gives them concrete form by transforming them into grandiose charitable institutions; a man of transcendent soul who binds the sublime ideals of religious fervor to the exquisite expression of beauty in art, thus giving new life, as if by magic, to the conception of piety and genius held by his ancestors; a man who understands the necessities of his times and struggles to gather around him a handful of intelligent, ardent, and dedicated workers; the type of good shepherd who lives the life of his sheep, mingles with the most humble of his children, is acquainted with the demands, the shortcomings, the character of each and every part of his vast and varied diocese, and does not neglect its most distant corners, but sheds his blessings everywhere; a man with the heart of the genuine philanthropist who strips himself of his all, even the most precious and cherished mementos to come to the aid of the afflicted; a soul full of holy exultation as he recalls the deeds of glory done for God and country. This is how Piacenza has come to know Bishop Scalabrini during the twenty-five years of his episcopate. (*The Life and Works of a Great Bishop*, by Monsignor Francesco Gregori, pp. 327-28.)

As such he now steps before us for recognition by our century and for the equitable judgment of the Church.

Bishop Scalabrini ended his days here on earth when sixty-six years of age, on Ascension Day, 1905, as though to participate in the triumph in heaven of His Divine Redeemer.

We trustingly await another Ascension Day, when Our Lord will call upon his priest and faithful minister to participate of his glory in the same Church to which he gave his all in the fulfillment of his apostolic and missionary ministry, even to the last offering.

✠ Fr. A. G. Cardinal Piazza

Bishop of Sabina and Poggio Mirteto
Secretary of the Sacred Consistorial Congregation

Rome, Septuagesima Sunday
February 14, 1954

CHAPTER 1

Under the Sun of Lombardy

*Lombardy . . . cradle of the
strong and the valiant . . .*

Bishop Scalabrini was a pure-blooded son of Lombardy, born in Fino Mornasco, a little village near Como. His parents were also both Lombards. His home was small and of modest means but not poor. The house faced the parish church which still stands today with the added attraction of a commemorative tablet to the Bishop of Piacenza.

His father, Louis, was a storekeeper well esteemed in the village for his honesty and his sense of the important place religion should occupy in everyday life. His mother, Colomba, had come from a nearby town and was one of those women who bring the richest of dowries to a home— wisdom and the holy fear of God. Two people such as these could hardly fail to bring blessings upon the family they brought into the world—five sons and three daughters. A certain prosperity was theirs and they succeeded in giving their children an honorable social position. The girls married into good families. The first son, Anthony, succeeded the father in running the business and did so well that the family's standing in the community was raised to a comfortable level. Two other brothers went to America. One died there and the other became a university professor and later the assistant mayor of the city of Paraná in South America. The youngest received the degree of doctor of philosophy and literature and was appointed inspector general of Italian schools in foreign lands.

John Baptist Scalabrini, the third child of the family, was born July 8, 1839. On the same day, as was the custom, he was baptized. On September 8 of the next year he received the sacrament of Confirmation in the same church.

The date of his First Holy Communion is not known exactly, but probably it was when John was still very young, perhaps even earlier than it was customary in those days. From an early age his mother had been his teacher and with true Christian spirit had instilled into his heart the knowledge and the love of God. His pastor, Father Philip Gatti, intelligent and dedicated, recognized the unusual qualities in the young boy and saw fit to prevent any obstacles from rising against his desire of receiving his Lord in the Blessed Sacrament.

Early in life John showed signs of an uncommonly brilliant mind and a keen sense of right and wrong such as to make people think that his life would be different from the majority of men.

The people of the village recall that John was not only active in gathering the children of his own age together, but also in teaching them the true meaning of religion. His pastor visualized the priest in the little boy, if perhaps not the bishop, as he watched him and listened.

These were not idle dreams. After ending his studies at the village school with high honors, John was sent to Como to attend high school and college where he distinguished himself among his friends and fellow students for the above-average qualities of his mind and for his irreproachable character. Among his companions were several outstanding young men who later became known for their brilliant careers. Some of these men were his constant friends through the years.

Although his parents hoped that he would become a priest, they wisely waited for God's established moment and placed no obstacles in his path. When their son decided to enter the seminary they welcomed the decision. Father Gatti seconded the proposal. At eighteen John entered the seminary to complete his studies, which at the time went under the title of Studies in Philosophy.

Upon completing them the young man went on to the Somaschi Fathers Institute, where he was also placed in charge of discipline. From here he passed to the Major Seminary, where he kept on with his studies and continued to distinguish himself in the sacred sciences as well as in other fields, principally in modern and ancient languages.

Bishop Bonomelli said of him:

"God had blessed him with a ready mind, versatile, keen, vast. He would have been successful no matter what course he chose to pursue, without any difficulty. The most profound questions on philosophy, theology, history, or political science were treated by him and developed with a certainty and an insight that were truly astonishing."

Also outstanding was his sound and profound spirit of devotion which merited for him the unconditional admiration of his superiors. Again the kindness and charity with which he was so prodigal inspired devotion from his colleagues who loved him as a friend and a brother, always ready to give and to sacrifice himself with no demands upon them of any sort.

In 1860 he was admitted to sacred orders and on May 30, 1863, he was ordained a priest. He was then twenty-four years old.

CHAPTER 2

In the Vineyard of the Lord

*. . . that the City of God
might be rebuilt . . .*

IN THE LITTLE VILLAGE of Fino Mornasco great celebrations marked the day on which the new priest, Father John Baptist Scalabrini, offered his first Mass.

It is not often that a parish has the honor of assisting at the first Mass of a young priest. When it happens, the people are usually deeply touched and not reticent in showing their feelings.

In the case of Father Scalabrini, added meaning was given the sacred ceremony, since the celebrant was the son of an esteemed village family beloved by everyone.

On that day the new Levite made his solemn entrance into the parish church. The sacred edifice was brilliantly lighted and crowded to the doors. Father Scalabrini was accompanied by godparents, according to the local custom. He offered that first Mass in the presence of his happy parents, relatives, and friends. After the Mass he received the greetings of the whole population.

Later, dissuaded by his bishop from leaving for distant places as a missionary, he set his hand to the plow without losing time in useless recriminations, exercising his sacred ministry part of the time in a parish church in the mountains and part of the time in his own native town, which was dear to his heart.

Later on his bishop, Marzorati, proved it was not chance

alone that had made him say: "I need you here." Only a few short months had gone by when the bishop appointed him dean of discipline as well as professor of history and Greek in the Seminary of St. Abbondio. Father Scalabrini distinguished himself so highly in fulfilling his duties that in 1867, when only twenty-eight years of age, upon the death of the rector, Father Angelo Bolzano, he was appointed to succeed him.

We need reflect only an instant on the importance and the delicate nature of such a position, charged with the molding of future priests, to realize the high esteem in which this young priest was held by his superiors.

That year an epidemic of cholera broke out and hit the province of Como very hard in many of its towns and villages. Among them was the town of Fino Mornasco.

Father Scalabrini never hesitated a moment as to the solution of any calamity, whether material or moral. Giving no thought to his own safety, he threw himself into the battle, offering help and assistance to those in need.

It must be remembered that at that time, almost one hundred years ago, medicine had not progressed to the point it has reached today, and so his work often meant placing his health and life in jeopardy. The young priest's work during that period was so outstanding that not only was it a source of edification for his confreres, but it also awakened deep admiration among the people. The civil authorities themselves recognized the value of his services and awarded him a Public Health Medal of Merit. Summer and autumn went by and with them the heat and the deadly disease. At the beginning of the following year Father Scalabrini was able to take up his duties as rector of the seminary, where he disappointed none of the hopes that had been placed in him.

"John Baptist Scalabrini," writes Monsignor Cattaneo, who spent several years at the seminary first as a pupil then as teacher, "had a tremendous intuition of the significance

of the times and of the ways of Divine Providence. Gentle of
mien, simple and dignified of manner, a perfect gentleman
in speech and decorum, he gave constant proof of quiet
strength, kindness of heart, loftiness of soul, and the integrity of a healthy and vigorous nature.

"With these assets, personality, and spiritual self-control,
he took up his duties full of confidence in God's assistance.
His straightforward glance and his authoritative counsel gave
a clear insight into the new horizons he had in mind. He
willed to fill the sanctuary with chosen souls and the Church
with holy priests, that the City of God might be rebuilt. This
was what he desired most in his heart and soul. It was his
faith, the goal of his whole life."

His constant care, therefore, was the improvement of the
means for the education of the young seminarians whom
he loved and by whom he was well loved in return. But he
tempered this affectionate regard with strong disciplinary
rules necessary if youth is to be drawn away from the bad
habits contracted in circles far different from seminary life.
He reorganized the course of study and personally taught
religion classes. These classes continued for many years.
They were of such tremendous help to the diocesan clergy
in the bitter struggle with the enemies of Christ and the
Church that an ecclesiastical group of young men full of the
spirit of faith and nourished by profound studies was forged
to add to the dignity and the decorum of religious life. He
also put in order the finances of the seminary which at the
time left much to be desired. These accomplishments
were noted by his superiors and at the death of Bishop
Marzorati, the successor, Bishop Carsana, appointed him as
assistant vicar general and member of various diocesan congregations. In discharging his new duties Father Scalabrini
distinguished himself for the fairness of his judgments and
for that practical sense which made him understand and

successfully solve difficulties as they arose, bringing his under-takings to successful conclusions.

His first meeting with Jeremiah Bonomelli and the sub-sequent strong friendship between these two men go back to this period of his rectorate at the seminary. Jeremiah Bonomelli was that "gigantic figure of a patriotic bishop who gave honor to the Church and to his native Italy as few other personalities of the nineteenth century have done."

Bishop Bonomelli was also a Lombard. Master of Catho-lic doctrine and of the true meaning of Christian Catholic thought, he was an austere and zealous shepherd. His tem-perament might be compared to that of a thoroughbred horse, ready at any moment to leap away, suddenly straining at the reins held too tightly, but with a heart and soul as simple and pure as that of a child. A productive, effective writer, a brilliant orator, an outstanding apologist, a sincere and passionate patriot, a fearless and most daring pioneer of a conciliation between Church and state, and a benefac-tor of exceptional qualities, proud as a lion, humble as a monk, a devoted son to the Holy Father, in youth and in old age, as a pastor and as a bishop, he fulfilled to the letter what Giovanni Papini, Italian writer, wrote of Pope Pius XI.

In fact Bonomelli as well as Achille Ratti, who was to be Pius XI, belong, as Papini states in one of his writings, to "that Lombard clergy that worked hard and well in a land where it may be easier even today to meet with a courageous cardinal than a cowardly priest. [This, of course, refers to the saintly Cardinal Federico Borromeo and to Don Ab-bondio, the weak-minded priest in Manzoni's famous novel, *The Betrothed.*] And he always remained such in the truest sense of the word a true Lombard, a man with an open tenacious mind devoted to his fatherland, both the great and the small, Italy and Lombardy, more inclined to action and reason than to building castles in Spain; also a man with high ideals of family life, courageous when courage was demanded of him, prudent in all things, modest without making of modesty an alibi for laziness or a cover up for fear of responsibility, cordial yet firm in his opinions, faithful to his ideals and to his friends."

The meeting between Bonomelli and Scalabrini is told by Bonomelli himself:

"In the year 1868 I was invited to give two separate series of retreats at the two Como seminaries, the major where theology and philosophy are taught and the minor for high school and college subjects. Scalabrini was there as rector and professor. I knew him only by name because of the good reputation he had won for himself through keenness of his intellect and also through his work as a zealous priest. He was then thirty years of age, if I am not mistaken. I was thirty-seven at the time and pastor of Lovere. We saw each other, we exchanged a few words, and immediately became friends. That friendship so true and sincere lasted unchanged until Scalabrini left this earth for his journey to heaven."

Undoubtedly here were two souls born to understand each other, two characters that complemented each other, two noble hearts that had come on earth to exchange strength and good counsel toward the accomplishment of great deeds. In 1871 Bonomelli was appointed bishop of Cremona and a few years later Scalabrini was sent to head the diocese of Piacenza. Providence placed them near each other and their meetings became more frequent, their friendship, if possible, closer.

"Between us," Bonomelli goes on to say, "there were no secrets. I think it would be difficult to find two friends who could have been more closely united than we were. And this friendship, although so close, never usurped or lessened our individual liberty of thought or action on any point. Rather this liberty made our friendship all the more enjoyable, more solid, and at times even heroic. Bishop Scalabrini gave me many a proof of this in the difficult moments of my life."

Theirs was indeed a happy and a holy friendship, founded on reciprocal respect.

This is the type of friendship which, according to the Book of Wisdom, is born and bears fruit only between "the good," and is rendered perfect only between "the best."

CHAPTER 3

Tricks of Providence

. . . with a Father's love . . .

IN THE YEAR 1870, after seven years of experience in the training of youth and three as rector, Father Scalabrini was assigned as pastor of St. Bartholomew's, one of the largest and most important parishes in the town of Como.

The management of such a parish consisting of 10,000 souls could hardly be considered a "demotion," but why was he removed from a position which he had fulfilled with such zeal and to the full satisfaction of all concerned?

It is told that on the eve of the Insurrection movements of 1821 a short poem in manuscript form on the martyrs of Italian independence was circulated among the seminarians. The incident caused scandal and astonishment among the faculty, since it looked like a hymn of praise to that movement which led to the taking of Rome. The scandal increased when it became known that the author of the poem was the seminarian Angelo Scalabrini, brother of the rector. It is superfluous to state that the rector was utterly in the dark, but after all he was the rector. It was up to him to tackle the problem. His position as superior and as brother of the culprit became extremely delicate. He tendered his resignation.

It may be pertinent here to say "too bad!" And yet it was Providence who really had a hand in this whole affair. Through this unfortunate incident this servant of God was placed more directly in contact with souls, and thus was the way paved for the road which had been traced for him.

Five years later he was consecrated bishop of a diocese

which boasted of three seminaries and 364 parishes! It was well and fitting that having trained himself in the guidance of future ministers of the Gospel he should also train himself in the duties of a pastor.

Father Scalabrini made his solemn entrance at St. Bartholomew's in Como on the third Sunday of July, when through an ancient tradition the feast of St. Aloysius Gonzaga is celebrated in that particular church. Father Scalabrini, even as a child and young man, had always had a particular devotion to that saint and had in fact written a poem in praise of him when only fifteen years of age.

The new pastor was received by a cheering crowd, and from that moment on Father Scalabrini's whole effort was put forth in being just a pastor who loves his people, cares for them, knows every one of them, and stands ready to give his life even for the least of them.

His first care was to promote and revive in his people the spirit of devotion, especially to the Blessed Sacrament and to the Blessed Mother. A man of deep piety himself, one who drew new energy and inspiration from his daily visit to his Lord in the Blessed Sacrament and from his acceptance of suffering, he longed to make his spiritual children partakers of the grace which filled his soul. From his daily meditations on the sorrows of Our Lady he was led to accept gladly any trials, whether physical or moral, which God saw fit to send him. He was assiduous in the care of the sick, comforting and caring for them, unsparing of himself, and for their sake forgetting sleep, food, and physical weariness. He lingered at the bedside of those in their agony, as a father watching a dying son.

Well versed as he was in theology and sacred scripture, and endowed with the gift of making them clear and simple to his listeners, he was as tireless in giving instructions as he was in gathering the fruits of the seeds he sowed within the con-

fessional where every day of the week numberless penitent
sinners and faithful flocked to him.

"With a father's love," writes Monsignor Cattaneo, "he
gathered to his heart all weaknesses and human misery. And
how many souls he brought back to his Father's house! This
occurred because of his loving solicitude which reached out
into every family, every institute, every factory, in one word,
into every class of society. . . ."

Father Scalabrini himself wrote:

"Among my parishioners I had hundreds and hundreds of
silkworkers, weavers, spinners, dyers. In those years I was
able to see at firsthand the miserable conditions under
which these people worked, miserable in themselves and miserable for their consequences. Each crisis, political or financial, which either increased or slowed up their work, the only
means they had for their subsistence, kept them in a state of
continuous worry and uncertainty. Those were sad days
when, climbing humble stairways, I failed to hear the rhyth-
mic hum of the loom!"

In the region of Lake Como every house resounds with the
beat of the loom. It is a sign of life. And if the loom is silent,
it may not be a sign of death, but certainly of poverty and
desolation. When the looms were silent, Father Scalabrini
knocked at the door of the rich, seeking help that they might
once again resound to their normal beat.

It is easy to understand how this way of life conquered all
hearts for him. One day, we are told, when Father Scalabrini
received threats against his life, his parishioners, fully armed,
surrounded the rectory and gave proof of being ready so that
not a hair of his head might be harmed.

At that time Catholic action was hardly more than a
pious and vague desire. Yet Father Scalabrini spoke of it
and practiced it, organizing groups of young men and
women, providing as much as possible for the welfare of the
working classes, initiating the first Mutual Aid Society built

on Christian principles and the first nucleus of the St. Vincent de Paul Society, whose purpose was to visit the poor and the sick in their own homes. He founded the Nursery School and we can learn how much care he showered upon this group by reading the *Small Catechism for Use in the Nursery Schools*, written by him and published in 1875.

The catechism! It is hardly necessary to tell him who is aware of today's world how many ills and disastrous results have been brought about by ignorance of the meaning of religion. It is needless also to bring into relief the fact that teaching catechism is for a pastor one of the most important duties. But if Father Scalabrini were to return to this world today he could well say: "I have no regrets," for the bishop who later on in his life merited from Pius IX the title of "apostle of the catechism" began even as pastor to dedicate his heart and intellect to the teaching of the catechism. He is one of the few men of his time who realized the necessity for a *vibrant, alive* system in teaching catechism such as would constitute a living food for the young, never realized by a parrotlike recitation of a long rigmarole of questions and answers. Thus in his own parish he made the first experiment in the reform of catechetical instruction which later would be his first act of government as bishop of Piacenza.

Not satisfied with all this, he also found time to plan the enlargement of his parish church. So intense and enlightening had been his pastoral life in the community that it had brought about a deep and rewarding awakening of the spiritual life. The church had grown too small for his flock. There was need for expansion. Father Scalabrini set out to get the necessary funds and to draw plans.

However, although he had to leave everything in a state of suspension on his consecration as bishop to the diocese of Piacenza, he never ceased to interest himself in the project, helping and spurring on his successors to fulfill what had

been one of his dreams. In gratitude for his great help a bust
of Bishop Scalabrini occupies a place today in the magnificent temple, more imposing because of his efforts.

In 1872, when he was still pastor of St. Bartholomew's,
Father Scalabrini was invited to give a series of conferences
on the Vatican Council in the Cathedral of Como. These
conferences were most appropriate to the time. The Council,
initiated on December 8, 1869, and suspended the following
July, because of the new political and military developments
which led to the seizure of Rome, was the subject of lively
discussions and bitter enmities, notably in what dealt with
the infallibility of the Pope, which had been proclaimed a
dogma of faith on July 19, 1870.

In the following year, 1873, Father Scalabrini published
these conferences in one volume under the title *Vatican
Council,* and dedicated it to his former colleagues and students at the seminary. A great crowd of listeners had flocked
to the conferences, there to give an attentive ear to the calm,
thoughtful words, free of any exaggeration. Intense had been
the attention of the faithful, intense also the sympathetic
reception from the general public. Stronger still and not less
favorable was the echo raised by his published book.

The Pope also read it, and this not by mere chance. It
appears that he did not hide his approval and pleasure. It
is said, moreover, that this book led Pius IX to raise its
author to the bishopric. Certain it is that only three years
were to pass before he became bishop of Piacenza.

At the time his friends and admirers, those who had been
embittered by the transfer of Father Scalabrini from the
seminary to the parish, had to come to the conclusion that
with our "shortsightedness" we may never pretend to measure the paths traced for us by Divine Providence.

CHAPTER 4

Shepherd of the Church

. . . gifted in youth, wisdom
and high purpose . . .

FATHER SCALABRINI, pastor of St. Bartholomew's, learned of his elevation to the bishopric in a rather curious manner. On the morning of December 17, 1875, he was in the church when an unknown ecclesiastic walked down the main aisle and approached him respectfully.

"Do you wish to offer the Holy Sacrifice?" Father Scalabrini asked with surprise in his voice.

"No, indeed," answered the unknown priest. "I have said Mass. I am here only to render homage to my new bishop."

Father Scalabrini stared, unbelieving. In thoughtful regard for his visitor he did not ask him to what nonsense he was referring. But feeling he had to get out of a difficult situation he said calmly:

"Come, Father, let us go to the rectory and have a cup of coffee together, and then you can return whence you came. But let us hurry, so that no one may even get an inkling as to the reason of your coming and take the thing seriously."

A few hours later, however, a letter arrived from Rome with the official communication of his nomination. In the meantime the news had swept the city.

Shortly afterward the newly elected bishop, in his first pastoral letter to his clergy and to the people of his diocese, expressed himself thus:

"At the unexpected news of my appointment to such a weighty position, knowing full well my lack of great virtues

31

and my immaturity of years, as well as the difficulties encumbent upon so high an office, I beg your prayers and your leniency. By the authority vested in the Blessed Vicar of Christ on earth I see this to be a manifestation of the will of God. Thus, trusting in the graces with which he bestows strength upon him who confers this solemn dignity, fearful of myself and yet trusting in him, I have submitted myself to the ministry imposed upon me. Far from any desire on my part to investigate the reasons for this honor bestowed upon me by divine goodness I am reassured by the firm hope that he who works within me both in will and in action will not fail in strengthening me, directing me, and lending me his constant help. . . ."

He then went on to delineate his program, giving his solemn promise that he would spare himself neither hardships nor sacrifices, that he might be as a father to the unfortunate members of his flock, teacher to the ignorant, leader of priests, and shepherd of all, thus to bring everyone to Christ.

The episcopal See of Piacenza, before the accession of Bishop Scalabrini, had been held for twenty-six years by Bishop Anthony Ranza, a native son, learned and full of wisdom, a man of deep modesty, piety, and singular charity.

Bishop Scalabrini, nominated in the consistory of January 28, 1876, was consecrated bishop two days later in the Church of the College of Propaganda Fide in Rome by Alexander Cardinal Franchi, the future secretary of state of Leo XIII. On that same day he addressed his first letter to his flock which has been mentioned before.

That same year also witnessed the celebration of the sixth centenary of the death of the Blessed Gregory X, and Piacenza, glorying in the fact that it had given him birth, readied itself to celebrate the date with unusual solemnity.

Bishop Ranza had given notice of this the previous year and all plans had been made and decided upon when on

November 20, 1875, almost at the very time when the celebrations were to begin, he suddenly died. The problem came up as to their postponement, or as to the method of procedure without the bishop.

This situation was courteously presented to the new bishop. A man of action, swift in settling matters, resolute and dynamic, Bishop Scalabrini had a quick intuition of the embarrassment in which the organizers of the solemnities found themselves, and only fourteen days after his consecration he made his solemn entry into Piacenza.

Plans proceeded without a hitch. The celebrations were fixed for the month of February, from the 13th to the 16th. The cathedral was resplendent. A huge painting of the Blessed Pope hung over the main altar. Twelve bishops and high prelates were present in the sanctuary.

The new bishop made his solemn entrance on Sunday, February 13. The day was brilliant, a fitting background to the success of the ceremony.

Young, tall, handsome, noble of bearing, imposing in his ecclesiastical robes, his glance intelligent and kind, the new shepherd won every heart. As he moved along between long, deep lines of the thousands who had come to welcome him, his hand lifted in blessing, a smile lighting his face, the enthusiasm of the people broke out in continuous applause.

Later, when he addressed them in the cathedral, his words, it may be said, vouched for his great success.

Many years had passed since the people of Piacenza had heard their bishop speak in the cathedral. The edifice was vast and microphones and loud-speakers were still only "in the mind of God." None of his immediate predecessors seemed to have possessed a voice that could fill it. Bishop Scalabrini, on the other hand, was the possessor of a strong, vibrant voice. The people of Piacenza were well pleased.

The four days taken up by the celebrations were a test of his mental and physical strength, but they were also days when the heart of the bishop and the heart of his flock beat in unison.

On February 16 the bishop celebrated his first pontifical Mass. The speaker that day was Abbot Placido Schiaffino, superior general of the Olivetani and a future cardinal. While his words were a panegyric in honor of Blessed Gregory X, he found time publicly to give praise to the new bishop. He defined him as "gifted in youth, wisdom, and purpose."

Many letters were received by Bishop Scalabrini, in which again and again he read that "in difficult times and in times which tend to worsen, a bishop such as you is sorely needed. . . ."

The festivities, successful and satisfactory to all, came to an end, and the new bishop went immediately to work. His task was far from easy, since the sharp conflict then existing between Church and state prevented him from occupying the official bishop's residence which the state had confiscated. Moreover, he could not accept the yearly compensation which the state had established for the bishops, without the express consent of the supreme ecclesiastical authority.

While Piacenza rejoiced, the parish of St. Bartholomew's in Como mourned. The departure of their beloved pastor had been considered a public catastrophe, and no one seemed able to resign himself to the new situation. It was felt that any priest who might be chosen to succeed him could never fill the place he had left vacant. His former parishioners always referred to him as their "pastor-bishop," and continued to keep him in their hearts.

The bishop himself never forgot them. Every time someone happened to come from Como to see him, he would hasten to ask:

"Anything new at St. Bartholomew's? Do crowds still come

to listen to the Word of God? And how is the recreational center getting along? What about the new church?"

The new church was the one he had planned, and he continued to consider it still his own—at least in a modest sense.

CHAPTER 5

At the Head of His Flock

. . . he observed, studied,
prayed, then provided . . .

Among the cardinal virtues we find prudence. This virtue is useful to everyone, but for bishops it represents quite completely a utensil of primary need. A bishop who through an absurd hypothesis might at the very outset of his official career set out to tear down and build up again whatever he finds, without first acquainting himself with his new surroundings and his new people, would give the impression of lacking in this virtue.

Bishop Scalabrini, on the other hand, proceeding step by step, disturbing no one and giving much time to thoughtful reflection before making any decision, showed himself as being prudent whenever or wherever this became necessary. But he did not stress the subject, for too much prudence may be taken to be a cover up for uncertainty, laziness, or fear. These defects, as we shall learn, the new bishop did not possess.

Hence he observed, studied, prayed, then provided. All was done without haste, for he was young, and time, God willing, was on his side. His first acts were a manifestation of the fact that beyond wisdom he possessed a highly spiritual nature.

The wise builder who is anxious to see a sturdy edifice rise story by story gives thought first of all to the ground on which the building is to stand and to the foundations. A bishop who intends to reawaken in his people the practice and fervor of a Christian way of life must begin by bringing his clergy to the top of spiritual efficiency, for is not the priest "the salt of the earth"? If the salt is tasteless, what can take its place?

His attention, therefore, focused itself immediately upon the priests, endowed with the full dignity and responsibilities of their high calling and upon those who were being trained toward the priesthood in the seminaries. He reminded them first of the importance of periodic spiritual exercises. Anyone not devoid of religious knowledge knows these to be a powerful and effective means in the healing of souls. He called for conferences to solve cases of moral theology. The purpose of these conferences was to maintain a lively interest in religious problems and to bring priests together in stronger bonds. He provided a reorientation of sacred studies and instituted new courses for the seminarians. He also appointed a fixed spiritual director, nonexistent until then, and gave precise directives in the teaching of philosophy, teaching which was to be based on the writings of St. Thomas Aquinas. Thus he anticipated what Leo XIII later ordered for all Catholic schools in his encyclical *Aeterni Patris* of 1879. All of this Bishop Scalabrini accomplished after extensive visits to the two seminaries and also to the Alberoni College. The latter institute had been founded by the celebrated statesman, Cardinal Alberoni, who was also himself a native son of Piacenza. The institute still continues to train young men for the priesthood.

His next task was to place the administration of the sacrament of Confirmation under strict disciplinary measures. For a long time this sacrament had been administered in fits and starts without regard to any pre-established plan or any definite criteria. In the major centers of the diocese the announcement that the bishop was coming to administer the sacrament would bring a flood of candidates for the reception of the sacrament, all of them gathered together pell-mell from any and all parishes of the zone. Even newborn babes were brought, for their parents felt this might prevent years of waiting on their part for the next chance.

Had not this also happened to Bishop Scalabrini himself when he was only a year old? This custom seemed to him, and in fact it was, far from being consonant with the dignity of the sacrament "which makes us perfect Christians and soldiers of Christ." As a result he fixed seven as the age at which Confirmation could be conferred. He also recommended that pastors in particular provide for an adequate preparation for any and all candidates. Finally he took it upon himself to administer the sacrament periodically in all parishes.

In the first year of his episcopacy Bishop Scalabrini also gave great thought to the "faithful departed." He notified the diocese of the special indulgences granted by Pius IX "so as to increase in the faithful the love of the holy souls and the charity involved in alleviating their suffering in purgatory." This "delicate thought" for the departed souls imparted a sympathetic note to the early days of his episcopacy and is a sign of that vibrant spirituality which is at the base of all his actions and his works.

In the meantime, every Sunday and during the week Bishop Scalabrini was to be found among his people, now in one parish, now in another. The pastors, knowing he would be pleased, often extended invitations to him to visit their parishes which he as often accepted. Thus it was possible for the shepherd to draw ever closer to his flock.

The great work which distinguished him most at the beginning of his episcopal career and one of the truly outstanding aspects of his personality as a man of the Church was his apostolate of the catechism.

Convinced of the vital importance of teaching and

strengthening Christian knowledge of the catechism and determined to make this widespread, the bishop worked for such an ideal which had already been realized during his pastorate at St. Bartholomew's. Only two months after assuming his duties as bishop he wrote a pastoral letter which he had outlined beforehand. In it he recalled the law of the Council of Trent on the teaching of the catechism. He referred in a special manner to the work done by the Blessed Paolo Burali along this line who, during his own episcopate, had instituted flourishing schools for Christian doctrine. With this as a premise, he explained the necessity incumbent upon every priest to dedicate himself to such teaching. Furthermore, he gave in great detail the necessary instructions as to how to proceed in the matter. The following summary of these instructions gives proof of his keen mind and his zeal.

Each parish was to have three classes for the children, more if possible, and one for adults. A society for Christian doctrine was to be founded which was to provide directors, teachers, and assistants. The pastor was charged with their training, since catechists are not improvised but molded. He added a set of rules to the letter by which he re-established the Diocesan Commission of the Catechism, and appointed directors for each deanery who had to pay periodic visits of inspection to the various parishes.

One of the prerogatives of this Servant of God was to engender obedience through love and with love. So much so that as soon as the pastoral letter was received, the pastors immediately set out to fulfill the given orders. In a short time the catechism schools were organized and flourishing in every parish.

The following year, on November 4, 1877, satisfied with the work done, he wrote a letter full of praise to the teachers of both sexes in the catechism schools, and added a papal brief in which the Holy Father praised their work and granted them a plenary indulgence on the anniversary of their joining the Society of Christian Doctrine, on a number of feast days during the year, on one day to be designated every year in each parish, and finally at the point of death.

In order to maintain the spirit of the apostolate alive and thriving, Bishop Scalabrini gave orders that the teachers in the city parishes were to meet once every month in the Church of St. Mary in Cortina, where he himself addressed them, unless unavoidably prevented. For country parishes he appointed a spiritual director of teachers, charged with visiting the schools.

In an appendix to the letter he furthermore announced the forthcoming publication of a monthly periodical, under the name of the *Catholic Catechist*. The first copy of this monthly came out on the following July 5. It was announced that the monthly had been placed under the direct management of a well-known psychologist of national fame, Carlo Uttini, and that it had been granted a special blessing by Pope Pius IX. The purpose of this periodical was to delineate the glory and the effects of Christian doctrine and to show how the teaching was to be adopted in the home, in the school, and in the church. It answered a need which had been felt for a long time. This was fully proved by the quick success it had in Italy and by the enthusiastic reviews it received in the Catholic press.

Not satisfied as yet, Bishop Scalabrini studied the text of the catechism then in use in his diocese, and wrote an accompanying text of instructions to be used especially in the training of teachers. Of this book an eminent member of the College of Cardinals had this to say:

"If the Bishop of Piacenza had done nothing else for his diocese, this book alone would be sufficient to make him an outstanding personality."

But Bishop Scalabrini did many other things. Each Sunday afternoon he visited a number of parishes which had

been notified beforehand, went from catechism class to catechism class, questioned the children, encouraged the teachers, and spoke to the people. He stressed the necessity that
all, especially parents, be instructed in religion and see
that their children be well instructed, too. In other words,
he gave instructions with zeal and he himself lived that zeal.

CHAPTER 6

Through Ways and Byways

*. . . trying to break the record
set by St. Charles Borromeo . . .*

ALMOST 200 of the 360 parishes of the diocese of Piacenza
are situated high on the hills, or literally on top of the
mountains. Today access to these places has been made
easy and comfortable. There are smooth roads, and swift
and modern means of transportation. But in the days of
Bishop Scalabrini the only means of getting there was on
the back of a mule or on shanks' mare.

This was a serious problem for a bishop who was anxious
to visit his churches and his pastors every five years, according to regulations. It was so serious, in fact, that his predecessors, prevented by age or by reasons of health from solving
it, had limited themselves to visiting only the nearby seats.
To faraway places they would send some young monsignor
to find out what he could and bring back any information he
could gather. Since the time of the Blessed Burali, that is,
almost three centuries before, certain small villages clinging
to the tops of mountains had never again seen a bishop's
skullcap.

During the first year of his episcopate the young energetic bishop re-established the custom of the pastoral visit.
He made evident his intention of paying a visit to each of his
parishes personally. And he kept his word. He started, according to custom, at the cathedral, where his visit was preceded
by a solemn mission, extending to the entire city. At its conclusion the bishop was rewarded in noting evident signs of

a religious awakening. On the feast of the Immaculate Conception he alone kept on administering Holy Communion for almost three hours. In memory of the mission, he instituted the pious monthly practice of a day of adoration to the Blessed Sacrament in the Church of St. Michael. This practice was particularly dear to his heart, dictated as it was by his burning love for his Eucharistic Lord.

During the winter he visited each of the city parishes. In the spring he pushed on into the countryside, and at the beginning of summer he started to climb the mountains.

Realizing that not a few of the country and mountain priests might be embarrassed at the idea of having to offer him and his suite food and lodging, he decided to establish his headquarters, as it were, in the deaneries. This was not meant for the reception of priests and people of the surrounding country as had occurred during the time of his predecessors, many years before, centuries in fact, but for the sole purpose of spending the night and then starting out early each morning on his journeys. Anyone could easily understand that this solution certainly did not lessen, but rather added to, any hardships he might encounter. And hardships indeed there were, not only for him, but for those who accompanied him.

He covered many miles on the backs of mules, he tramped along on foot, he leaped across mountain streams, he clambered up rocky mountain paths, challenged the rain and storms. Nothing held him back. Once, when he had to reach a village over three miles of mountainous paths, a furious storm broke. His priests begged him to halt and interrupt his journey, or at least to wait until the storm abated. He refused, donned the winter clothes of the local pastor, straddled his mule, and set out, led only by the thought of a patient people waiting for him. He knew they were awaiting him under a lashing rain.

As soon as he arrived at any small town, if confessions were to be heard, he entered the confessional immediately, especially if men waited, and if necessary sat there for long hours.

His days saw a continuous succession of active work, without a moment's rest. He wanted to see everything, take cognizance of all things. Wherever he stopped, he preached —at mass, after imparting the sacrament of Confirmation, during conferences on the catechism, at cemeteries. There were times when he gave ten talks in one single day! He visited the sick, listened to the humblest of his flock who approached him with confidence and filial trust, interested himself in their affairs, sad or happy as they might be. The right word, which encourages, convinces, placates, never failed to rise to his lips. Rich or poor, it never mattered to him to whom he spoke. Children were his special delight. They surrounded him joyfully, attracted by the charm of his smile and his personality.

Once, tired out after a long ride, he came to a mountain parish where the pastor, a very old man, met him with unexplainable coldness and indifference, making no move even to offer him some small refreshment. His priests were indignant, but not a word passed the lips of the bishop. He accepted a bowl of hot soup offered to him by a kind person and went on with his work.

"He is trying to beat the record set by St. Charles Borromeo," said his co-workers.

True, Bishop Scalabrini had made up his mind to follow that saint. In fact, he had initiated his visits on the feast of St. Charles.

The following is given as the opinion of Monsignor Tedeschi, one of those who accompanied the bishop:

"The hardships borne by the bishop are excessive. If he continues at this rate he will shorten his days."

This was indeed true.

The *Corriere Piacentino,* a periodical far from favorable to the Church and the clergy, gave recognition in spite of itself to his tireless efforts. Disturbed by the success of the missions initiated in preparation for his pilgrimage throughout his diocese, and by the manifestations organized to give honor to the bishop, this daily publication had flung itself at him, calling his efforts "public fanaticism." Against its own will it was forced to recognize, although far from graciously, that Bishop Scalabrini was indeed working with "incredible dedication."

What counted for a man of the fiber of Bishop Scalabrini and what is most uplifting to anyone who appreciates and venerates his memory is the clear, unbiased fact that any effort he put forth for the glory of God and the lifting up of men's souls obtained the desired goal. He obtained it in so definite a manner that good people were both edified and stirred toward a better way of life.

The periodicals of the day state that the number of sinners returning to God was considerable. Scandals were corrected, illegitimate unions were regulated, hatreds put aside and forgotten. What this "Messenger of God" brought about by his very presence, his work, his priestly powers, could be called a veritable tidal wave of grace. Few could resist him, few opposed him too long.

The words he spoke, the enthusiasm he aroused sufficed to cause new churches to be built where there were none or where they were too small or too unworthy. But it must be remembered that before renewing the temples of mortar and stone he saw to it that the souls of men, the temples of the Holy Ghost, were rebuilt and made less unworthy.

On September 26, 1880, he declared his first pastoral visits ended. With good reason he could say that he was comforted by the thought that he had become acquainted with the whole of his diocese, even to its remotest corners. He had a *Te Deum* sung in all of his churches, a hymn of thanksgiving for the work accomplished through the help of God.

CHAPTER 7

A Cross and a Chalice

. . . opposition and recognition . . .

Pius IX celebrated his episcopal jubilee on June 3, 1877. This was a good occasion on which to manifest to the saintly pontiff the feeling of solidarity and affection felt by those of his flock who had not proved unfaithful to him.

Bishop Scalabrini, who throughout his whole life had a deep and abiding devotion for the Pope, gave solemn notice of the auspicious occasion and announced its celebration in all the churches of the diocese, urging especially the reception of Holy Communion. He exhorted the faithful to this, to pray that the love in the heart of the great pontiff not only be strengthened by the love of his children, but that God Almighty would bless him of His very strength. Then on June 7, he left for Rome, at the head of a large number of pilgrims from his city and diocese. He was granted an audience with his flock and on that occasion the Holy Father presented him with a pectoral cross of rare beauty.

"The cross of a bishop is precious," Pius IX said to him, "but it is a heavy cross, heavy rather than precious." The truth of these words was soon to be experienced by the young bishop in their full meaning!

Upon his return to Piacenza he was able to take possession of the bishop's residence, freed from the decree of royal confiscation. On this occasion he received enthusiastic greetings, and there was good reason for rejoicing but no reason for illusions.

A bishop as zealous as he was, dynamic, believed in by his

46

people, of whom it was said that he obtained whatever he wished, could not escape from straining the nerves of the enemies of the Church to the breaking point. The powerful Freemasons, especially, angrily and vindictively awaited their chance for a propitious occasion to arise that they might destroy his prestige and, if possible, knock him down from his high pedestal. The occasion presented itself on January 9, 1878, the date of King Victor Emmanuel II's death.

Here it behooves us to recall briefly the historical facts of that period. We must remember that the seizure of Rome had occurred only seven years previous, that the King had been excommunicated, that the relations between the Holy See and the Italian state were as yet very tense. The bishops throughout Italy were prohibited, except when authorized by Rome, from promoting or taking part in religious ceremonies which might have any political significance.

When questioned about provisions for funeral services in honor of the dead King, Bishop Scalabrini, not having received the necessary disposition from Rome, answered that he could not at the moment make any pronouncement.

Honest and loyal persons should have immediately recognized the reason for the bishop's delay in giving a more satisfactory answer to them. But the interviewers had no sooner left the bishop's residence than they began to spread the false rumor that the bishop had refused their request for funeral services for the dead King. Thus, the rumor continued, he had placed himself openly against the national political situation then existent. In other words, they denounced the bishop as being anti-Italian. At the time this was the accusation in vogue in Italy, which made its way into the mind of the masses, easily swayed in their opinions by clever and unscrupulous propagandists.

The false rumor immediately was believed in spite of its untruth and stirred up a wave of indignation worthy of a better cause. The city seethed with excitement.

On January 19, Bishop Scalabrini was peacefully returning from one of his pastoral visits when, while crossing one of the city squares, he noticed people standing about in groups. As he reached one of the main streets he was forced to drive between large crowds of people who, instead of greeting him, as was their usual custom on seeing him, ignored him or cast sullen glances upon him.

"A storm seems to be brewing," he said to himself.

In fact, as soon as he reached his residence boos and cat-calls were heard on all sides. Insults were hurled at him, and then the crowd broke through the gates and into the court-yard of the residence. There it stood, until guards and the police arrived, far from promptly it must be admitted.

By this time the fuse had been lit. Demonstrators rushed to provoke disturbances under the windows of well-known sympathizers with the Church and with the bishop, people dubbed as clericals, then proceeded to the seminary, demanding that the national flag be flown at half-mast. Finally returning to the Cathedral Square, they sought to pull down the bishop's coat of arms. The police had to charge them and scatter them.

On the twenty-third of the same month Bishop Scalabrini, saddened by the occurrences, but firm as usual, wrote his pastoral letter in which he clarified matters. His words unmasked his detractors and strongly vindicated his right of being faithful to his own mission by obeying his legitimate superior, the Supreme Pontiff. And then from Rome came the welcome permission for funeral services to be held in honor of the dead King. The bishop had not given in to lay pressure, and now with the supreme ecclesiastical authority on his side, he not only gave his permission for the funeral service to be held in the cathedral, but he himself offered the Mass in his pontifical robes.

At this gesture full of dignity and fraught with meaning, the people not only were pacified but they repented, apologized, and rallied around him. Devoted to him more than ever, they were embittered against those who had tried for their own ignoble purposes to alienate them from their bishop.

Pius IX, as a sign of his complete approbation, sent the bishop a gift of a golden chalice crusted with precious stones.

The chalice was sent on February 6. On February 7, to the extreme sorrow of his great Catholic family, Pius IX, the mild, kindly Pope who had sat on the throne of Peter through many difficult years, was summoned to his reward.

Bishop Scalabrini had loved him as pope, but loved him, moreover, for not a few personal reasons that rendered Pius IX particularly dear to him. He willed that his memory be honored in all the churches of the diocese with prayers both public and private. A solemn funeral Mass was offered in the cathedral. Finally, to give lasting form to the gratitude and admiration he and his diocese felt for the former Pontiff, he planned to dedicate a monument and a religious school to his memory.

The project for the school, in spite of all his efforts, did not materialize. His other project, however, was rapidly successful, and within three years a marble statue of Pius IX was unveiled in the cathedral.

CHAPTER 8

A Golden Page

. . . sell thy goods . . .

O N FEBRUARY 20, 1878, Cardinal Gioacchino Pecci was elected pope. He chose the name of Leo XIII.

Bishop Scalabrini hastened to give the good news to his flock and shortly afterward he left for Rome to pay his homage and that of his people to the new pontiff.

On that occasion he begged permission for the building of an institution which lay close to his heart. His wisdom as a bishop and the scope of his vision were confirmed by the words he spoke.

In Rome stand ecclesiastical colleges of various nations, destined to gather within their walls chosen elements, presumably called to fill posts of responsibility and command. Here priests come to perfect themselves in sacred studies by frequenting institutes of higher religious learning. To Rome, center of Christianity, seat of the Vicar of Christ, they flock to absorb the Catholic and apostolic spirit of the Roman Church, a spirit they will in later years pour into the minds and hearts of the brethren whom they will be destined to teach and guide.

Bishop Scalabrini was fully cognizant of the advantages offered by these seats of learning, advantages that give the Church that spiritual union which constitutes one of her fundamental characteristics. For a long time he had nurtured the wish to reopen the Lombard Seminary in Rome, a seminary which years before had been opened for the identical purposes as the colleges founded for the use of the foreign clergy in Rome. In 1870 it had been closed principally because of the complicated political situation.

Now he wanted to give reality to his wish and see the institute not only once more set aside for the priests of Lombardy, but destined for the benefit of priests from all of northern Italy. He wanted it to be not the Lombard Seminary but the Northern Italy Seminary.

He spoke of his project to many. Among his listeners was Cardinal Borromeo, former head of the Lombard Seminary. The cardinal approved of the project and charged Bishop Scalabrini with making the opportune contacts with the bishops of the regions involved in the project. This was done with Bishop Scalabrini's usual alacrity.

He conferred with Duke Thomas Gallarati Scotti of Milan, who had been the chief and almost the only benefactor of the seminary. Difficulties arose, especially where money was concerned, but, nothing daunted, the bishop set to work and solved them. On November 4, 1878, he had the great joy and satisfaction of seeing his dream realized. On that day the new institute was inaugurated and at the ceremony he had the well-deserved honor, not only of presiding, but also of being the official speaker.

True it is that later on, due to an unjustified attitude taken by the rector with regard to certain students who were accused of professing Rosminian ideas, Bishop Scalabrini, jealous of his clergy's reputation, and as always bold in the face of injustice, refused to send any students from his diocese. This incident, however, does not dim his merit in the efforts he put forth for the reopening of the institute.

In the meantime Bishop Scalabrini continued to fulfill gradually the program he had laid out for himself as bishop. In 1879 he published several pastoral letters. Among them there is one which is considered important. It discussed the subject of the benevolent influence exercised by the Catholic religion in society and served as a commentary to the papal encyclical *Quod Apostolici Muneris.*

His work never ended; his visits kept on. In 1879, after intense and meticulous preparations, he held a diocesan synod. This had not taken place since 1723.

The same year is especially remembered in the life of Bishop Scalabrini because "one of its pages, truly enveloped in golden light," brings into sharp focus another aspect of his noble spirit.

Torrents of rain had fallen unceasingly during the whole of the spring season and had caused great damage to the farmlands in his diocese. By June the weather cleared and persisted clear throughout the whole of the summer, inaugurating a dry spell so long and so complete that in spite of the spring rains the little that remained of the crops was utterly destroyed. Agriculture was in a state of ruin. Industry and commerce faced a tremendous crisis. Winter came—an unusually bitter one. Poverty was general. In the country many of the farmers were forced to beg for alms. In the towns there was no work to be found. Prices soared. Vital necessities were unobtainable. The situation was extremely serious. One harsh word defines it—hunger!

People accustomed to a life of ease and decorum suffered. The poor, bewildered, and starved were a pitiful sight to behold. Refugees from the country—men, women, and children—poured into the cities in search of aid, and reduced life to a spectacle of tragic drama.

Facing the threat of famine, which day by day grew in horror, the bishop did not hesitate. He was convinced that if he were powerless to crush it, that did not prevent him from daring to use all the means at his disposal to attack it. This he did.

A passionate appeal poured from his lips to those he knew to be filled with the real meaning of Christian charity. To their generosity he added his own, and transformed the first floor of the bishop's residence into an enormous kitchen. Therein he installed the Sisters of St. Anne who worked countless hours, preparing warm soup and food to be distributed to the hungry.

On December 11 the daily papers announced that throughout the month of February one thousand bowls of soup would be distributed daily at the bishop's residence. But the number of the hungry kept increasing. One thousand bowls of soup became two thousand, then three thousand, and finally four! But hunger was not the only specter knocking at the door. Freezing cold weather hit the region. The poor were barefooted, half-naked; they had no bedcoverings—perhaps not even a bed. The bishop was far from satisfied with asking and begging from those who had to dig into their well-filled coffers for the had-nots. He opened his own. They were far from well filled, but he stripped them bare.

The day came when all resources seemed to have vanished. His own means were exhausted, and the Sisters advised him that on the morrow the fires in the stoves would go out. For a moment Bishop Scalabrini was desolate, but only for a moment.

In those days every bishop was given horses for his own private use. The bishop sold his horses and the money went toward keeping the fires burning in the kitchen stoves. The profits from the sale disappeared and still the winter and the misery that it brought were not over.

In his private chapel inside a small closet there stood a golden chalice adorned with precious stones. Around the stem of the chalice were three figures representing the Father, the Son, and the Holy Ghost. It was the gift he had received from Pius IX.

The bishop looked at it. Had it not been perhaps a gift to his people? The giver, then, would certainly not hold it against him for giving it back to his people. He sent for a jeweler. The chalice changed hands. The bishop received a sum of money. . . .

As a result starving people now had food to the last day of the great famine.

At a session of parliament one of the members spoke these words:

"We, also, should do something. We cannot permit the bishop of Piacenza to have a more charitable heart than we, a bishop who distributes thousands of bowls of soup a day to his poor. Before that priest, gentlemen, I bow my head in veneration. I admire his sublime sense of the apostolate, and if all priests were like him, I would become one myself."

On the anniversary of Bishop Scalabrini's consecration, January 30, the whole population of the city honored him by sending a message wherein its gratitude and its praise were made public. It was signed by thousands and thousands.

Everything possible had been accomplished and the situation was becoming normal again. Then the Freemasons in Piacenza, who had been forced to join in the bishop's triumph, did their utmost by innuendos and by articles in their daily paper to prove that the initiative for saving the people from starvation was not the bishop's, but that he had embellished his own character only with other people's sacrifices.

Later, in an article written for the newspapers by the General Aid Committee, the full truth was told. The bishop made no comments, but everyone realized that the bishop had been the most conspicuous donor throughout the time of need.

CHAPTER 9

Winged Charity

. . . charity the greatest . . .

THE PREROGATIVE OF MEN inspired by apostolic zeal and the charity of Christ is to widen their scope so as to embrace any problem which may in any way touch their brethren. They consider these problems as theirs, particularly if they regard the unfortunate and the sorrowful.

At the time when Bishop Scalabrini was still pastor of St. Bartholomew's in Como, he had become the close friend of Father Serafino Balestra, promoter of a charitable organization for the deaf and dumb, and propagator of a purely oral method in teaching these unfortunates. Bishop Scalabrini had collaborated with him as director of the institute which was under the care of the Canossian Sisters.

Spiritual father of the deaf and dumb . . . as such Bishop Scalabrini wished to be known. To this office he had passionately dedicated himself. As he studied the condition in which these poor should find themselves, "so solitary among men," almost as if they could be called "abandoned men in a silent wilderness," he was led to consider the more tragic side of their existence, that of being prevented from having any contact between their soul and their God.

This preoccupation continued alive within him when he became bishop. On September 8, 1880, he wrote a pastoral letter wherein he treated the subject and brought the attention of the public to these unfortunates. He spoke of them as "souls starved for spiritual food, men and women outside the fold as it were, ignorant of revealed truth, even the most necessary and elementary." He stressed the point of how easily they could be exposed to the greatest of moral evils, subject to the predominance of the senses. "Falling into sin, it would not be a simple matter for them to free themselves, deprived as they are of any means of grace, or of the knowledge of the supernatural life."

It was clearly evident that he meant to face this problem. It was clear also that God was certainly on his side. In fact, one day he heard that a young deaf-mute utterly devoid of any means of support was being held by the police, until such time as a place could be found to shelter him. Bishop Scalabrini immediately offered to take him into his own house.

The authorities were deeply grateful. A letter written by the bishop to the prefect of the province makes it very clear how much he was doing along that line. In fact, he wrote that quarters for girls were almost ready and two Sisters, trained in this special work, had been installed there. A young woman instructor from Siena, deaf and dumb herself, had joined them. The bishop had high hopes that an institute for boys could be opened later.

In order to prevent any objections which might arise from the suggestions that institutes for the purpose were existent, he faced the problem.

"True," he wrote, "an individual here and there might be provided for, as the case arose, but then the actual need would soon be forgotten. With an institute in our midst the attention of the public would be focused on the problem. Public and private charity would join together to provide for the present as well as for future needs. Thus the civic, moral, and religious life of these many unfortunate souls would be assured.

"Let me point out," he concluded, "the fact that by your objections we would deprive ourselves of one of the finest achievements with which our city might bring glory upon itself."

Somehow or other the bishop overcame all the difficulties that as a rule rise up in the path of such initiatives especially those of an economic nature. Toward the end of the year 1880 the girls' institute was beginning to function. Its first and provisional home was inaugurated in 1881 under the name, Institute for the Deaf and Dumb. Leo XIII honored the project by providing funds.

The founder had expressed confidence that Providence would not fail in seeing that the work was brought to completion, and he had been right. As long as he lived, the institute aided by generous benefactors, well known and anonymous, grew and prospered. It continued to prosper after his death, so much so that it became possible to increase the number in its care. Later it was legally incorporated.

On the other hand, Bishop Scalabrini was unable to provide personally for the Institute for Deaf and Dumb Boys, but even in this profound hope of his he was not to be disappointed. Monsignor Torta, one of his collaborators, had never forgotten the words the bishop had spoken to the pastors in 1880, with regard to the sad situation of these unfortunates. In August, 1901, he told the bishop that a boys' institute for the deaf and dumb was to be inaugurated. A long-hoped-for dream was to become a glorious reality.

CHAPTER 10

Frangar Non Flectar

. . . my honor . . . the solid
strength of my brethren . . .

I MAY BE BROKEN, but I shall not be bent." This should
have been the motto inscribed under Bishop Scalabrini's
episcopal coat of arms.

Under the episcopal coat of arms rather than over, as he
was so living a proof of its inflexibility that it appeared as if
he had assumed it as a prerogative of his concept of the dignity of a bishop and the great duties inherent thereto rather
than a characteristic of his temperament. That is to say, he
held this inflexibility as a necessary requisite of the shepherd.

The reader will realize this more and more in the following
pages. Here are related the many vicissitudes and unpleasant circumstances and occurrences which took place in the
last quarter of the nineteenth century. These are facts
which, due to the many intervening years, and considering
the passions that provoked them as well as the men who provoked them and the men who were their protagonists,
should be referred to with due objectivity and the spirit of
charity required of us.

Two things must be held in mind if we are to draw a fair
evaluation of the facts about to be related: first, the struggle
then existing in the philosophical and theological fields between the Thomists and the Rosminians; second, in the political field between the Intransigents and the Transigents.

The Thomists stressed the importance of restoring the

philosophy of St. Thomas Aquinas in all the Catholic schools. The Rosminians sustained the ideas of the philosopher-priest from Rovereto, Father Anthony Rosmini.

The Thomists drew their strength and, justly so, from the directives given by the then-reigning pontiff, Leo XIII. From their point of view the Rosminians quoted from Pius IX, who had defined Rosmini as a man of "the highest wisdom, most obedient, most exemplary." On the other hand, up to that time no judgment had been passed upon the theories held by Rosmini by the supreme ecclesiastical authority. Only in 1881 did Leo XIII condemn "the forty propositions" taken from Rosmini's writings. It may be added here that this did not prevent St. Pius X from declaring Rosmini to be a "saint."

The Intransigents were those who demanded the total restoration of the temporal power of the popes. The Transigents opposed this idea. When Rome was seized from the popes, the Intransigents sustained the theory that it was impossible to come to terms with the usurper. The Transigents were of the opinion that in spite of the fact that they disapproved of the extortion, to call it such, it would be wiser to accept the *status quo* and come to terms as in any war. They supported this course for above all other considerations it would not cut the Church and the Catholics off from the national life of Italy, a possibility which at the time was beginning to show signs of definite growth. They argued their position on the basis of the principle that absentees are always in the wrong, since they always end up by getting the worst of any bargain, even though they may be in the right.

The Intransigents were made stronger by the rigid hands-off attitude assumed by the Holy See. Their opponents held to the fact that politics is not a matter of "faith and morals." They firmly believed they could not be prevented from attempting to bring about a solution of the painful problem.

Of course they also subordinated their decisions to any from Rome. They hoped, however, that the attempts on their part might hasten the necessary understanding by the people as well as bring about the helpful action by the Church which seemed so dangerously near being cut off from the life of the Italians.

Two problems, one philosophical, the other political, each clearly distinct from the other. Distinct and yet continuously intermingling in the heat and the battle of contrasting passions. Such confusion ensued that the Thomists and the Intransigents were knitted into a single block against the Transigents who were labeled Rosminians by their enemies and, as such, denounced and bitterly fought.

In this state of affairs the best way out should have been the application of the sound principle expressed by St. Augustine: "Unity in what is necessary, liberty in what is doubtful, charity in all things." Sad to say, however, it is difficult to sift out the whole truth when the battle rages. The victim is always charity.

The flag-bearer of the conservatives (Intransigents) was Father Davide Albertario, who had all the good qualities, but also all the usual defects, of the "spearhead." Enthusiastic, aggressive, fearless of temperament, one who for the papal cause, as he understood it, was willing to face the hangman's noose and who handled his pen now as a sword, now as a cleaver. His writings were characterized by a spirit of extreme aggression. He imposed his will by daring. However, many times his aim was poor.

In Piacenza at the time a certain narrow antagonism existed between the former pupils of the seminary and those of Alberoni College. As has been said before, the latter was a great institution but was pointed out as being too much in sympathy with the Rosminian philosophy. Thus it is easily explainable why the former leaned toward the articles by

Father Albertario, champion of extreme orthodoxy against the presumed danger of the Rosminian theories. It can also be understood why some people regarded Bishop Scalabrini with a suspicious eye, since he was not disposed toward an agreement with their discriminatory criteria.

It so happened that some of these for the mere pleasure, we believe, of needling the Alberonians wrote an article in the *Osservatore Cattolico* (the paper whose editor was Albertario), attacking an article published in the Alberioni periodical, *Divus Thomas*, which, incidentally, was by Bishop Pio Del Corona of San Miniato. The attacking article stated that the concept of the Thomistic theory therein expressed was not true, but, worse still, it insinuated that it could hardly be otherwise since it had been published at the Alberoni.

The bishop, sensitive as he was to the upholding of truth, could not remain silent. He wrote to Father Albertario expressing his displeasure at the attack. Albertario knew full well that he could not number the bishop of Piacenza among those who agreed with his point of view, much less with his methods. He answered that he regretted having displeased him. Nevertheless, a few days later he did not hesitate to oppose him further by publishing a report in which he rather vulgarly attacked the bishop's secretary.

An old Tuscan adage says: "I speak to my daughter-in-law that her mother may get the point." Bishop Scalabrini, understanding that things might be carried too far, cut the matter short and dropped his subscription to the paper. He added that he "forgave him and prayed that God might point the way of true wisdom."

Relations between Bishop Scalabrini and the *Osservatore Cattolico* were at this stage when the bishop relieved the seminary rector of his duties, the rector having expressed a desire for a change of position. The matter was of no exceptional importance. It is a well-known fact that a member of the faculty of any seminary is under the direct juris-

diction of his bishop, who can make any changes he may
see fit to make. However, since this particular rector happened to be a member of the editorial staff of the *Osservatore
Cattolico*, the followers of Father Albertario immediately
saw in his removal a reason for charging the bishop with ulterior motives. They felt that the cause for the removal was
the desire on his part to appoint men with views which were
contrary to those held by the Intransigents. It may be superfluous to add that the *Osservatore Cattolico* sounded the
alarm on this note, as if in the diocese of Piacenza the
Pope's cause was literally in danger as well as the orthodoxy
of the Catholic Church.

The truth of the matter is that Bishop Scalabrini was far
from being a believer in the Rosminian theory, although he,
as many others, prominent men of the Church among them,
admired for his intelligence and holiness the zealous and
exemplary Father Rosmini, who had died more than twenty
years before. It may be said that in a fatherly way and prudent as a shepherd should be, the bishop tried to understand
the priests in his diocese who leaned toward Rosmini's theories without openly antagonizing them. By such a method
he hoped that, having obtained their respect and trust, he
might later induce them to the necessary act of obedience
and acceptance, in case the Rosminian theories were to be,
even in part, condemned by the Church. This seemed fairly
certain at the time and later did take place.

Along with his great friend Bishop Bonomelli and other
important prelates Bishop Scalabrini favored conciliation
between the Church and state. He maintained that an attitude of rigid protest would be most damaging to the
Church itself. The enemies of the Church, in the opinion of
these men, could very easily use this rigid attitude, change its
purpose to suit themselves, and attempt to prove the Church

an enemy of Italy, and so succeed in alienating some of the Italian people.

The struggle between the Church and the Italian state troubled him deeply and he hoped for a solution. Not for a moment, however, did he forget that all his ideas were to be subordinated to the directives from the Papacy. Never did he harbor the least thought of opposing papal directives even though they might have been contrary to his own convictions. These could not keep him from fulfilling his duties as a believer and as shepherd of the Church.

Strong in this knowledge and this loyalty, Scalabrini was as strong in his inalienable prerogatives as bishop. Subjected to underhanded and unworthy attacks, he kept silent for a long time.

When he saw that his friend, Bishop Bonomelli, was undergoing the same fate and the same attacks, and when these attacks became a distinct campaign of defamation, he decided that silence had to be broken. On October 3, 1881, he published a vigorous protest in the diocesan paper, *The Truth*. The article was a model of pastoral dignity. After declaring himself "above those ever-deplorable quarrels which arise between parties," and in the full knowledge of the "formidable judgment he would one day have to face before God as his judge," he wrote a strong protest against the dangerous insult the *Osservatore Cattolico* had hurled against the Pope through his own humble person. From St. Gregory the Great he quoted the following words:

"My honor is the honor of the Universal Church. My honor is the solid strength of my brethren. Then only am I honored when honor is not denied anyone to whom honor is due."

He thus vindicated the honor of his clergy, that many a time had been pointed out in the columns of the *Osservatore Cattolico* as Jansenistic, "while we," he added, "bless

God for having placed us at the vanguard of a chosen group of priests. Their spirit of sacrifice, their zeal, their abnegation, and their profound sincere submission and attachment to the Supreme Pontiff and the Holy Roman and Apostolic Church is to be praised. We can assure the Holy Father that they accept and will always accept his decisions, no matter what they may be, for the present or for the future."

He protested against the undue interference of the *Osservatore Cattolico* in matters regarding his own diocese, declaring himself responsible only to the supreme head of the Church, "never to anyone who attempts to impose himself and to confuse in a sacrilegious manner the lawful order established by our divine Lord, Jesus Christ, on earth."

He concluded by affirming that while he was ready to impose appropriate ecclesiastical penalties upon anyone of his clergy who was guilty of writing articles meant as an insult to the ecclesiastical authority, he was at the same time ready to forgive all injuries and offenses directed against his poor person.

Bishop Scalabrini's energetic action brought about a tremendous reaction. The daily press printed comments upon it. The clergy of the diocese stood in a solid body with their bishop and showed their gratitude to him for having defended them in so authoritative a manner.

In the meantime, Bishop Scalabrini, seeking advice, sent copies of his protest to the papal secretary and to other ecclesiastical authorities. From Rome came an order to the *Osservatore Cattolico* to make amends. The answer given by the *Osservatore Cattolico* was far from satisfactory to the bishop. He wrote directly to the Pope. In his letter he asked for a detailed public apology and insisted that it should contain the fact that an apology was demanded not to Scalabrini, the man, but in all justice was due to the bishop, who had been insulted and abused.

Then in 1882, in order to clarify further the painful

occurrence, the bishop went to Rome. He returned with the assurance that everything would be done according to his request. Later, however, he received a rather evasive letter from Cardinal Jacobini. This letter induced him to pen a page which even today, so many years later, cannot be read without stirring our deepest emotions.

After stating that an expression of regret in general terms is not sufficient to protect the honor and the dignity of a shepherd of the Church, he textually states: "Here is the absolute necessity . . . either I must justify myself or be justified. To advise me to keep silent in this case would only mean adding insult to injury. It might as well be that 'it matter not whether the episcopal authority be flung in the mud.' This would give credence to the current rumors that an occult government by dishonest men is making people afraid, for they feel it is impossible to restrain them.

"A doctor of the Church would raise his voice in protest and cry out: 'Beware!' and he would add: 'Religion must beware when bishops are forced to keep silent.'

"Your Eminence, am I in error? Tell the Holy Father, then, to correct me and he shall find me always a son submissive and obedient in all things. But if I find myself, as I do, on the side of truth, justice, and right, then how can it possibly be permitted that a bishop, even the least and the most humble of them, be led publicly to a court presided over by a priest?"

In answer to this letter, respectful and yet peremptory, the Holy Father appointed a commission of six cardinals to "examine all the facts that had forced the bishop of Piacenza to file a protest against the *Osservatore Cattolico*, and to give their enlightened and impartial judgment." This was done. As a result, Father Albertario was given orders to apologize and retract unconditionally, as well, in the most explicit manner possible, the articles appearing in the *Osservatore Cattolico* against Bishop Scalabrini, on the ground that "they involved an undue and subversive influence and interference in his diocesan administration"

Justice had been done. If anything were to cause wonder in us, it should be the fact that Bishop Scalabrini had to expend so much energy in obtaining it. The reader should be prevented from any misunderstanding on the matter of the disloyal attitude about which Bishop Scalabrini speaks in the letter referred to. The thorny problem was that in "high places" certain dishonest men were imposing their will so as to make it impossible to restrain them. It may be opportune here to place in relief the fact that the Holy See so slow in its actions as, at times, to seem timid, finds its justification in the very position which had been taken by Father Albertario. As has been said, even taking into consideration his evident faults, far from negligible, he occupied a place of leadership in the bitter battle for the defense of the Pope and his sacrosanct rights, and to friends and foes alike he had become a symbol.

What repercussions would be brought about in both camps by a public retraction by this priest? Was there any doubt that such a retraction would weaken his whole course of action and paralyze an army, as it were, in the full heat of battle?

These questions must have weighed heavily upon the decision from Rome, resulting, of course, in a lengthening of the time taken in promulgating it. Anyone who has any knowledge of the situation, and we feel no obligation of dwelling upon it, must admit that both sides of the question had to be weighed in the balance and seriously evaluated.

This does not in any way, however, diminish the seriousness of the cause for which Bishop Scalabrini was struggling; nor his complete right in trying to see that justice be done.

To have fought so tirelessly to the very end justifies the admiration and the praise that he received. Men have always turned toward the desert, attracted by a voice that rises against injustice, but not for the mere sake of finding there "only a reed shaken by the wind."

CHAPTER 11

Like Tree Like Fruit

. . . generous, attractive,
brilliant . . . we must oppose this
formidable enemy with all means.

WHAT WE HAVE STATED at the close of the preceding chapter was proved true when on August 9, 1883, barely two months after the act of retraction had been imposed upon Father Albertario, Pope Leo XIII sent Bishop Scalabrini his portrait with a Latin dedication written in his own hand.

On the other hand, those who "could not" give homage to his courage prudently kept silent.

Bishop Bonomelli, a target himself, and vituperated against without mercy, wrote him a word of caution, placing him on his guard: "The skies are clear now, but let us beware and hold no illusions. Our eyes must be kept open."

At the beginning of the following year Bishop Scalabrini was forced to admit in a letter to his friend that "those particular people" were beginning to lift their heads again and that in all probability they were ready to make those responsible for the order of retraction pay dearly for their temerity.

In fact, a libelous article had been currently published under the title of "The Moth in the Church at Piacenza." In it the anonymous writer accused Monsignor Celli, the administrator of the diocesan seminaries and of the ecclesiastical funds, of improper conduct. It was easy to see that the real purpose of the article was to hit much higher up.

It is to be admitted that face to face with an exhaustive documentation written promptly and vigorously in refutation of his article the anonymous writer withdrew his statements. However, upon learning who was defraying the expenses, the bishop decided that nothing could be done save to follow the advice of his good friend and keep his eyes open.

This precautionary measure was indeed the right attitude to take.

In a small mountain parish of Bishop Scalabrini's diocese an incident had occurred which had brought about a quarrel between the board of trustees and two well-to-do families of the parish. Under the pretext that the church was in need of repairs, several pews had been removed and thrown in the nearby canal.

It was nothing of great importance, but the anonymous writer seized on it to write another libelous article. This article bore the title of "An Arbitrary Decree by Bishop Scalabrini and Its Consequences." It expanded the innocuous incident with childish insinuations and truly ignoble and false statements.

A lawyer who had great admiration for the bishop took the bull by the horns and exposed the writer, a poor man with neither money nor dignity, and induced him to confess that he had been sadly misinformed. Furthermore, he asked for the identity of those for whom he was working. Thus what had already been suspected was brought out into the light of day. The instigators of the libel were ecclesiastics, members of the faction heading the *Osservatore Cattolico*.

Later the same lawyer succeeded in learning from the same source that everything would be calm and peaceful if the bishop were to remove Monsignor Celli from office. This was the equivalent of having the bishop admit that the accusations against a man he himself had appointed were true. It was clearly a trap. His adversaries hoped that by falling into it, his lack of judgment in making appointments would be made clear and hence his hypothetical Achilles' heel be exposed.

Bishop Scalabrini was not the man to fall into the trap. Self-controlled as ever, and proceeding with his usual common sense, he told his lawyer to go ahead and give answer. If the charges against his administrator could be proved, he would be grateful to anyone who might give him the proof or even the information that might lead him to uncover the proof of guilt. He added that he would be glad to order an inquiry into the whole situation.

"However," he wrote, "I shall never sacrifice a good ecclesiastic on groundless charges for the sake of gratuitous and inadmissible hatred of people such as his accusers seem to be.

"Let them keep on writing. God will see that justice be done. And I shall also trust in the course of human justice, although at a previous time I was prevented through my desire for peace and charity."

He was offering everyone new proof of that moral uprightness and integrity as well as of that Christian courage which are characteristics of the shepherds of Christ and render resplendent the sanctity of the Church.

Was it possible that the avowed enemies of religion and of the clergy, aggressive and implacable in their purpose, were allowing their power to be surpassed by domestic enemies? Even to think this would be doing them an injustice!

Spearheaded by *Il Piccolo*, a biweekly paper of Piacenza, the Freemasons' battle against Bishop Scalabrini was proceeding on its way and was developing fast.

Of the 104 editions of *Il Piccolo* published in 1884, 43 carried articles attacking the bishop. It is interesting to learn the reason for such implacable attacks from a source admitting of no doubt. This reason was made clear from the minutes of a meeting held by the Freemasons and which came to light through a strange and providential means.

"The most powerful enemy of our society in northern Italy," read the minutes, "is Mr. Scalabrini, bishop of Piacenza. With his generosity, his attractive personality, his brilliant mind, he has imposed himself on everyone and everyone follows him blindly. Three of our brothers died and they were profaned by Church rites sung over them and we were boldly prevented from honoring them with ours. The Piacenza Lodge, so active at one time, has now been almost ruined through his machinations. We must oppose the work of this formidable enemy with all the possible means at our disposal and destroy him in the full Masonic sense of the word."

In truth, from their point of view we must admit they could hardly be blamed.

That Bishop Scalabrini abominated the sect and that he had given it no rest was well known. He had even had the courage to say so to a member of the government, an openly dedicated Freemason. On one occasion he personally went to the bedside of a dying dignitary of the sect on whose night table lay a revolver "with which to blow out the brains of any priest who dared to enter his room." How Bishop Scalabrini entered no one knows. The fact is that he succeeded in persuading the man to reconcile himself with his God. In consequence, the guards posted at the house of the sick man were dismissed on the ground that they were no longer needed.

This incident was the probable cause of the bishop's receiving a threatening letter, bordered in black, with the words "Five more days" printed in large characters. Bishop Scalabrini ignored the letter and continued to battle.

The act of accusation in recognition of his episcopal work in the minutes we have quoted seems to us to be the best homage he could have expected from his enemies.

Certain words of praise, however, demand a heavy price. We can easily imagine how Bishop Scalabrini must have been bitterly convinced, because of unmistakable signs, that the enemies on both sides of the fence had joined forces in order to reach an identical goal.

"It is an ill wind that blows no one good" is a proverb of truth. At a certain point the diocese, disgusted by what it had learned, reacted as one man, and launched its "enough" against both factions in a towering wave of indignation. Both the clergy and the lay population wrote to the bishop. They gave expression to their devotion which had deepened because of the degrading war being waged against him. All those letters were kept as a public reference. Finally, on December 7, the vigil of the Immaculate Conception, a commission composed of members of the clergy, the secular and regular, gathered at the bishop's residence and presented him with a pectoral cross and crozier as a sign of their love and devotion.

Hardly a month before he had written to his good friend and companion, Bishop Bonomelli, and had expressed himself in these words:

"The good God has deigned to visit me this year with physical suffering and moral vicissitudes. May his holy will be done in all things and for all things. I do not know what was written in *Il Piccolo* and by whom it was written. But no doubt some terrible things must have been said if I am to judge from the reaction of the clergy and the people. They are giving me proof of extraordinary affection and trust and they are prepared, from what I hear, to give me other proofs. As far as I am concerned, I assure you that I pay no attention to what is going on, but keep on treading the road traced for me. I bless God's holy name in the midst of these trials, certain that he will know how to draw some good from them.

"As for those responsible, it seems to me you are not far from the truth. The two Freemasonries are joining hands; we must be prepared. Victory will be ours, infallibly ours."

The miscreant engaged by the Masonic paper to defame the bishop ironically signed the articles with the name "Father Just." But faced with the indignation of the outraged clergy and public, he finally had to lay down his pen.

Although the bishop had come out of the struggle with a lofty spirit, his body, already weakened by the hardships of his pastoral work, suffered still more from the acute mental tension. He became ill and had to leave Piacenza for a period of rest and cure.

Bishop Bonomelli wrote to him jokingly and begged him to be in no hurry to leave for Paradise as "greater trials" awaited him. The bishop answered him that he had decided to modify the system he had formerly followed, confident that the thought of all the sufferings he had undergone might serve to render him more cautious.

Contrary to this, upon his return he proceeded to act precisely as had been his usual custom. And it was not long before he had to submit to the consequences.

"At a certain point in my sermon," he wrote to his friend, "I felt so ill that I had to stop in the middle of it."

A short, significant comment ensues:

"We must bend our heads before the judgments of God and supply for the deficiencies of our physical strength by sanctity. And I do have so little of it. Pray, then, for me. . . ."

Again he had to submit to a period of recovery. The result was so satisfying that toward the end of the year he could consider himself completely well.

Letters of congratulations came to him from every part of Italy. A letter from Cardinal Nina read:

"May God be praised! From the time I learned to my great sorrow of your serious illness I never stopped begging our Divine Lord to save a life so precious to us. . . ."

We shall presently see, even more clearly than we have seen so far, how truly precious that life was.

CHAPTER 12

A Papal Brief

*. . . face to face with
his public . . .*

THE STRUGGLE between the Intransigents and those who
stood for conciliation between Church and State, that
is, the Transigents, continued bitter as ever. Moreover, it
was not one of those struggles which could be stopped
merely by the promulgation of a law.

Convinced of the sanctity of the cause for which they
were fighting, the defenders of the Pope saw in anyone who
stood against their ideas a traitor against the Church as
well as the Pope. Their good faith in this cannot be doubted,
and yet they fought with such relentless fury that often
their blows were hurled madly about; so rather than aiding
the Pope's cause, they were harming it. The Holy Father,
instead of praising them, was forced to restrain and reprove
them.

A typical example of this situation can be gathered by
reading a letter written by Bishop Scalabrini to Cardinal
Pitra, sub-dean of the College of Cardinals, in the year 1885.
The cardinal was a scholar, completely dedicated to his studies in paliography, and lived, as it were, in almost complete seclusion from the world. He wrote that he was very
much disturbed in learning that part of the clergy and of
the people seemed unable to see, as he saw, the triumph of
the "antichrist" in the passing of the temporal power of the
Papacy. Continuing in this view, he went so far as to include
a mass of personalities, both living and dead, Italians and

foreigners, who differed from his views, and hurled himself against them in a manner totally unrestrained, qualifying them all as "enemies of the Church."

The person of Cardinal Pitra was worthy of respect, but his utter lack of prudence was too colossal not to have sad repercussions. Leo XIII saw himself bound to deplore the writing of the letter and to reprimand those Catholics who had spread it to the four winds. He showed his displeasure at their abusive use of it "almost as if they thought themselves authorized to act within the Church as its governing body, rather than its subjects."

Cardinal Pitra, brought face to face with the true state of affairs, retracted his words promptly and publicly, thus giving proof of his good faith. Others whose faith was not so "golden" did not do likewise.

Indignant at the use and abuse which the letter was continuing to bring about in Lombardy, Bishop Scalabrini wrote to the papal secretary. He stated that if the Pope were not averse to his idea he would be willing to debate the argument in public, and submitted an outline of what he wished to say. The cardinal answered readily and agreed that a pastoral letter on the subject might be opportune. Bishop Scalabrini did not need to lose any time in thinking over a subject which for so long had been a burning question in his very soul. In a few days his letter was in Rome "for approval."

Within five days he received a reply. The letter had been read and studied by the Pope and permission for its "go ahead" had been granted.

Bishop Scalabrini did not wait for a second invitation. The letter produced an enormous impression in Italy and beyond its borders. The press, whether Catholic or otherwise, discussed it. The *Osservatore Romano* reported it almost in full, and many cardinals sang its praises.

The Intransigents suspected the letter had a higher origin. They understood that Bishop Scalabrini, daring, but always most proper and prudent, would never have discussed the topic, hot as it was, unless he had provided for himself a strong wall upon which to lean for support. The letter was too decisive in tone not to point to this. They kept their lips sealed.

On November 3, 1885, the bishop went to Rome to confer with His Holiness concerning a new project which he had in mind and which not only had been brought to his attention, but had in fact been planned for him in very high places. It dealt with the writing of a pamphlet, under the title of *Transigents and Intransigents—Observations by an Italian Bishop*. Shortly thereafter the pamphlet was published. It was anonymous, as had been decided beforehand. Father Albertario launched his attack against editor and publisher alike.

"A bishop," he wrote, "cannot possibly have written such fantastic nonsense."

What would he have said had he known what Bishop Scalabrini affirmed many years later? It was no longer necessary then to make a mystery of the fact that the pamphlet had come "from the papal pen, not from his own."

At the time of the writing of the pamphlet Bishop Scalabrini had been obliged to keep his peace. It was far from easy for him to do so, for he had to admit that most of the attacks against the editor really should have been hurled at him. The editor, after all, was guilty only of having done him a favor. Attacks were also made against Bishop Bonomelli who, many were saying, should take upon himself part of the responsibility. The archbishop of Bologna also came in for his share of attacks for having authorized the printing of the pamphlet in his city. Bishop Scalabrini wished to take all of the blame upon himself. Leo XIII, although he understood the delicacy of his feelings, nevertheless counseled him against it, for the time being, at least.

"Whenever," the Pope wrote to him on January 7, 1886, "you should feel for any reason whatsoever, such as to protect the name of any person who may have suffered from any undue publicity, that you must make your name known, you are at liberty to do as you desire. I am depending on your wisdom to consider what unpleasant consequences to yourself such a revelation might bring about."

Bishop Scalabrini read between the lines as to what was clearly the wish of the Pope and bowed his head in submission. In recognition of this, the Holy Father sent him a brief in which, among other things, he assured him of his deep and abiding affection.

It was impossible not to understand that the pontifical document was directed to a bishop who was generally taken to be the author of the manual *Transigents and Intransigents*. It is not too difficult to imagine its consequences. But the legitimate consequence, which many years later is still full of great value, is the fact that the motto "for the Pope and with the Pope" was for him not only a slogan to boast of, but also a reality to live by, a duty to perform and, in time of need, a sacrifice to be borne with faith and charity.

CHAPTER 13

"I Seek Not Myself"

. . . cursed be thou who
kept silent . . .

THERE IS A TIME for silence and a time when he who is in
charge of souls must speak out that he may not deserve
the condemnation of the Holy Spirit, "Cursed be thou who
kept silent."

Bishop Scalabrini, as the reader must have learned by
now, was not the man who would remain unheard when he
felt he should speak, even though keeping silent might have
been simpler and perhaps more remunerative.

In 1886 the time came for the general elections in Italy.
Catholics were still prevented from going to the polls, as a
sign of protest against the Italian Government, called the
usurper of the rights of the Holy See.

But among Catholics there were those who were frankly
worried about the threatening progress of the political parties
opposed to the Church and the Pope. These men and
women asked themselves if it were wise to continue in this
passive attitude against the unleashed campaign waged by
their adversaries. Was this not playing at their very game?

It is superfluous to add here that Bishop Scalabrini was
one of these.

Since 1882, together with Bishop Bonomelli, he had written to Rome along these lines. Later he had discussed the
matter with the Holy Father. At this conference he had
spoken of the necessity of permitting Catholics to go to the
polls. He had also added that this procedure seemed to offer

a way out for, in his opinion, it would protect the Holy See from any danger or eventual uprising which might be fomented by excited and angered Intransigents. The Pope was deeply impressed.

The problem rose again and it needed an urgent solution. In Piacenza the candidates of the anti-clericals ran three to one against the others.

A number of the Catholic laity went to Bishop Scalabrini and asked his advice as to what to do. The bishop put the problem to the Holy See.

Monsignor Boccali sent an answer. It stated that no change had taken place since 1882, but when occasion should arise he could take advantage of private decisions received from the sacred penitentiary.

The private decision in this case stated that "with due reservations, matters could be allowed to run their course."

On the basis of this authorization the few who came to the bishop for advice and only these were told that, although the old order continued to function, the fact of going to the polls did not *per se* constitute an illicit act on their part.

However, a few among those who heard the bishop's words threw caution to the four winds and unfortunately gave little weight to the delicate position in which the bishop found himself. They doubtlessly held to the opinion that what was right for one was right for everyone. Means were found to let as many as possible know the happy news that Catholics could vote without risk to their eternal salvation.

"If that's the case," they thought, "who would wish to remain away from the polls when the political situation here in Piacenza is so precarious?"

Almost contemporaneously an article appeared in the paper, *L'Amico del Popolo*. The article was written by a priest, and in it the situation we have mentioned was discussed. The conclusion was arrived at, that not to vote was a great mistake, and that Catholics, by absenting themselves from the polls, would make a grave mistake. By voting they would do a great deal toward holding back the threatening flood.

Bishop Scalabrini was away on a trip and heard nothing of all this. But would it not have been next to impossible to convince the anti-clericals, the Freemasons as well as the Intransigents, that he was in the dark about whatever had occurred?

The former and the latter saw in him the astute puppeteer, intent on maneuvering his puppets as he willed, cleverly pulling the strings and having them move as he pleased. They turned against him, running a race as to who could find more abuse to fling at him.

The uproar which ensued did not limit itself to throwaways and newspaper articles. The Intransigents went so far as to appeal to the Holy Office itself, denouncing the bishop for an open infraction of the papal laws and demanding that immediate steps be taken against him.

The denunciation was too grave and too serious, too definite, not to have repercussions.

On his return to Piacenza the bishop found a letter from Monaco Cardinal La Valletta, secretary of the Holy Office. The latter wanted to know how much truth there was in the statements which had been referred to him, that "he had not only declared and made others declare that it was licit to go to the polls, but that he himself had promoted a campaign to that purpose and that he had, moreover, enlisted the aid of his parish pastors."

Bishop Scalabrini answered, dotting his "i's" and crossing his "t's," as he was accustomed to do, with documents at hand. He also wrote to the Pope directly, protesting against the insinuations and the accusations made against him by the *Osservatore Cattolico*, and declaring himself ready to defend himself publicly, before his own flock at least.

The answer to his letter counseled him against the action, as it would certainly not have succeeded in appeasing the two factions in conflict. The Pope's admiration for him, proof of which had been given to him more than once, should be sufficient to compensate him for the undeserved attacks! . . .

The letter had been written by Cardinal Jacobini. In his answer the bishop made the following statements:

"For that praise I shall always owe eternal gratitude to His Holiness. However, the praise does not compensate me for the evil opinions others are formulating against me. I am not seeking honors, nor am I looking after one as wretched as myself. God is my witness to this. I have delved deep into my own conscience, and I know that I am working for a cause far more noble and holy."

In the meantime the defamers continued their provocative campaign against him in the *Osservatore Cattolico*.

"I cannot keep from defending myself," the bishop then stated.

He immediately sent the Pope a report which he intended to give to the clergy. The Holy See again exhorted him to keep silent. The moment was tense. It can easily be understood. The instructions which had been given to him in a completely private form could not be made public without running the risk of incurring reactions and pronouncements which at so difficult a moment had to be prevented at all cost.

Bishop Scalabrini himself saw the point, and gave up his plan. From Leo XIII he received as a gift a volume of his poetic works, a proof in the gift that the Pope wished to make him understand that he had demanded so many sacrifices from him only because he had complete faith in him.

In 1887 the bishop wrote a pastoral letter to his people, entitled "Catholics in Name and Catholics in Deed." It had wide repercussions. In it he mentioned in detail the various categories of those who were Catholic in name only, and did not fail to point out also those that "not content with being subjects, as is their due in the Church of God [the phrase is the Pope's own], think they can assume a part also in its government." He qualified their system as a new "kind of liberalism," pharisaical and anarchical, which was all the more dangerous because it was beautifully camouflaged.

Bishop Bonomelli echoed these thoughts in his pastoral letter, "Liberalism and Its Mistakes," in which he gave the Intransigent Party all it deserved!

A formidable "pair" indeed! So great, in fact, that the *Osservatore Cattolico* rose in fury. Unable to launch a frontal attack, it attempted to strike at the flanks.

In that very year Abbot Antonio Stoppani, priest, writer, and scientist, who had been flayed for months at a time by the same paper, lost all patience and sued it for libel in the penal court of Milan. As witnesses he mentioned Bishops Scalabrini and Bonomelli. For motives of prudence the two asked to be excused. The defendants, however, must have feared the deposition of the two eminent ecclesiastics, for they mobilized all of their Roman friends to prohibit their appearance in court. Who knows what they were plotting?

The fact remains that Bishop Scalabrini received a letter from Mariano Cardinal Rampolla, secretary of state to His Holiness, in which he was advised that the Pope had no intention of granting "neither to him nor to any of his colleagues" the faculty of presenting himself at court, and hence asked him to do all he could possibly do to prevent it . . . which meant "doing . . . exactly what he had already done!"

As a result, the intrepid bishop wrote an answer, which even to this day holds us breathless. We feel that it must be given in order not to run the risk of presenting the bishop as having been "purged" and thus "crippled" and made "only half a man." Here it is:

"As I have always deplored the fact that a system of shameless accusations against bishops, clergy, and honorable citizens of the laity be tolerated, so also do I deplore the fact that a priest should have seen fit to recur to a civil court in order to uphold his honor. A knowledge, even an elementary one, of canon law, as well as the first elements of Christian prudence, a quality and a knowledge we attribute to a bishop unless we wish to offend him, might have led me to inform the Holy See of the message I received on the eighth day of the current month, if I had not immediately decided not to appear as a witness. To this effect I wrote to the civic authorities who understood the serious reasons involved in my decision. These reasons will serve for other bishops also.

"As you can thus well understand, Your Eminence, there was no need of informing me that the Holy See does not permit me to appear in court.

"A bishop who is neither a child nor an idiot asks for needed directives and always deplores being denied something he did not request!"

Who has ever said that the Church prohibits giving reasons for our actions? All that we need is the ability to state our case.

In fact, there is no evidence that Cardinal Rampolla sent any answer.

Those, on the other hand, who kept on talking were "those tongues from Milan," who continued insulting both bishops, even during the trial. The accusations were so flagrant that Bishop Bonomelli was forced to deny them in the *Messaggero*.

Bishop Scalabrini sent another letter to Rome asking whether it would not be wise for him to do likewise. Cardinal Rampolla advised him against it, but at the same time assured him that the Holy See would not fail to go into action at the close of the trial.

At least the necessity for taking certain provisions was recognized even where things were seen—from very high places indeed.

CHAPTER 14

True Greatness

*. . . indestructible strength of
the Papacy is wholly moral . . .*

In 1887 Italy was swept by a wave clamoring for conciliation between Church and State. Wise and honest men of different tendencies agreed in thinking that the cleavage existing between the Church and the government of Italy in 1870 caused by the seizure of Rome was at the time helping neither one side nor the other, and that in the interest of both a quick remedy was necessary.

There were those who held that the Italian Government should ignore the Vatican completely. Others felt that there should be a rigid adherence to the Law of Guarantees. The Vatican rejected this law as unilateral and oppressive. The legions of Transigents grew apace. They proposed a treaty granting the Pope true and individual sovereignty, *de jure et de facto*, with all the prerogatives attached to its meaning and connected with it, plus the possibility of exercising it in the most complete independence.

This was the solution which Leo XIII had personally, yet openly, foreseen and, let us add, the one which was sanctioned by Pope Pius XI in the year 1929 in the Lateran Treaty. But the time we are speaking of was back in 1887!

Bishop Scalabrini along with Bishop Bonomelli and many other important personalities of the day were, of course, among the supporters of this idea, one which history has proved to be the correct one.

As a man who knew what he was after and one who had an innate feeling of being on the right track, Bishop Scalabrini wrote to the Holy Father, wherein he expressed his own thoughts on the subject, thoughts which happened to be the same as of those "who love the welfare of the Church in a sincere manner, but who do not always have the courage to say what they feel deep within their own souls."

He began from the premise that outside of a veritable miracle the restitution of the temporal power to the *status quo* existing before 1870, that is on September 20 of that year, was possible only through the use of material forces or moral strength. These two hypotheses were equally impossible to realize. He asked the question:

"What is to be done to solve this intolerable situation, which, if allowed to go on longer, will only bring about a fearful future for the Church and for society? It is not the case of recognizing as such what occurred in years past, nor of proposing undignified solutions for the Holy See. The only solution is to find a way which at long last will promise a better future."

After stating that it was absolutely necessary to try to persuade the Italians that the Pope did not, in any way, want the ancient division of Italy, he pointed out that it would be wise:

1. To allow political elections to run their course, following a broad-minded program that tended only toward the general moral and religious good of the country.

2. To let it be known that Catholics want to act loyally along legal lines, interested only in the common good.

3. To permit good men to be members of the Senate and to increase the number as well as the courage of those who were already members.

"The indestructible strength of the Papacy," he continued, "is wholly moral and is even greater than in the past. This, therefore, should be the unshakable basis of its independence. Let us try to increase this strength throughout the world. Thus shall we prepare for its material restoration, which may take shape according to ideas made possible by changing times."

And he concluded: "To will the temporal power now, in all of its integrity and in its ancient form, is absolutely impossible. It can, as such, seriously endanger Catholicism in Italy. Temporal power is simply a means, and the means should not risk the end.

"I have wanted to say these things, not for the purpose of giving advice—may God forbid!—but simply to follow my conscience, which, in any case, will have your word as its irrefutable law."

Today, upon reading these words, we find it almost impossible to believe such wise words could be so bitterly opposed. We are forced to conclude, and this not without a feeling of regret, that if they had been understood, the good cause would have gained the ascendancy in Italy as far back as half a century ago.

We must remember, however, that ideas are like good fruit. One season is not sufficient for sowing them, nurturing them, and bringing them to maturity. Let us look back and render due homage to those who labored, plowed the soil, sowed the seed, and cultivated the tender plants.

In the Consistory of May 1887, Leo XIII himself declared:

"May God grant that the zeal for peace toward all nations which fills Our hearts may be beneficial to Italy in the only way We must feel to be the correct one. This is a nation that has been closely knit by God to the Roman Pontificate, and which nature itself binds so close to Our heart. We certainly, and for many years, have been hoping that once and for all the unfortunate misunderstanding with the Holy Father may be definitely removed, always, of course, according to the laws of justice and the dignity due the Apostolic See."

Evidently the Pope was on the side of conciliation along with Bishop Scalabrini. It was clear that he wished to feel out the terrain. The fruit itself was still far from being ripe.

Freemasonry rose up against his words, twisting their meaning to suit its purpose. In Catholic circles also malcontent was noticeable, that is among the ranks of the Intransigents, as if it was felt that the Pope had allowed sentiment to force his hand and had gone too far in permitting concessions that would be detrimental to the Roman See. In the meantime, in Vatican circles it was thought prudent to wait before further steps were taken, or decisions made.

This delay should perhaps have warned Bishop Bonomelli, who was planning to debate the question in an article, that it might be wiser to suspend its publication. Bishop Scalabrini advised him to do this, accustomed as he was to consider matters more realistically. At times, in fact, he had not hesitated from speaking frankly to his friend, even though by doing so he might hurt him to the quick. But Bonomelli, optimistic and impetuous as he was, thought the moment was ripe "for striking while the iron was hot." He gave the green light to the publication of his article first in the *Rassegna Nazionale* of Florence, the organ of the Transigents, and then in booklet form under the title *Rome, Italy and Reality—Thoughts by a Roman Prelate*. This treatise is still famous in the annals of the Roman question.

The booklet, written anonymously, in substance offered the Pope the Trastevere, the Città Leonina, and a strip of land extending to the sea, in evident contrast to the ideas held by Leo XIII, who was firm in his will to have the City of Rome. The booklet gave rise to furious outbursts. The name of the bishop of Cremona was bandied about as the author of the booklet. Its condemnation followed.

Bishop Bonomelli, on the advice of his friend, had immediately sent an anonymous retraction to the newspapers. He was uncertain whether to declare himself publicly as the author of the booklet or make known his name to the Pope in a private communication. However, as soon as he heard of the condemnation, and read his name in the papers as the suspected author, he no longer hesitated.

It was the day before Easter. On Easter Sunday he was to offer the pontifical Mass in the cathedral and deliver the Easter sermon. In that cathedral, standing erect in the pulpit after delivering the sermon, face to face with a huge crowd of worshipers, and in a steady voice which barely betrayed his intense emotion, he made the following declaration:

"I am the author of *Rome, Italy and Reality.*"

Then he continued:

"A soldier must obey his leader and so I also must obey my supreme leader, the Holy Father. As soon as I read his letter condemning my booklet, written anonymously, I hastened to write my act of submission, likewise anonymous. It was published in the daily papers. Last night I heard that it had been placed on the Index on the nineteenth of the current month. I should consider myself guilty, and more guilty than all others, since I am a bishop, if I delayed even for a day in making my public submission and in offering due reparations. What I said in my booklet, what I promised, I loyally maintain. Promptly, honestly, and totally, as a devoted son, I submit myself and my booklet to the judgment of the Holy Father, in whatever manner and meaning he may desire. I accept the condemnation, sorry for having afflicted him, and humbly begging his forgiveness.

"How could I demand obedience from my flock and my clergy were I not to walk before them in good example? I should condemn myself with my own condemnation. I take comfort and rejoice that by this public retraction here today, before my people and my clergy, and especially before my beloved seminarians here present, I can show them how to obey the supreme head of the Church."

The impression produced by this courageous act upon the people and the clergy was such that even today the mere mention of it sounds like the occurrence of a historical event.

Bishop Scalabrini was asked by the bishop of Cremona to act in his behalf with the Pope at Rome. On that same day the bishop of Piacenza sent the Vatican all the documents relating to the matter. He also sent a letter explaining Bonomelli's delay in revealing himself as the anonymous writer as soon as the Holy Father's letter had become known. He stated that the bishop of Cremona had acted thus so as not to bring upon himself any favorable opinions which might have been offensive to the Pope. And he added:

"This last act of his honors him more fully than all of his other great works."

To his friend he sent the following message of congratulations: "The history of the Church can forget many things you have done, but this, never! I am more than proud to claim your friendship."

A few days later Leo XIII, in a noble "brief," confirmed his trust in Bonomelli.

In reality such a declaration made by a bishop who was one of the most outstanding of his time, on Easter Sunday, from the pulpit of his own cathedral, is to us so great an act of loyalty, a genuine proof of Christian courage, that we are tempted to say: "O *felix culpa!*"

But the whole sad story does not end here. Other acts of true greatness were still needed before it was to be over, and thank God they did not fail to come.

The "misfortune" which had struck Bonomelli lessened for a time the attacks by the Intransigents against Bishop Scalabrini. Their target was the former, for they firmly hoped that he might be induced to abandon his diocese. Once he was out, they could settle with his friend. But the two friends were too closely knit not to present a single front. Any single attack upon either would find both men ready for the defense.

Bonomelli's enemies gave him no respite and sought to wear him down. They wanted him out of circulation at any cost. And they almost succeeded. Strong and vigorous though he was, he was about ready to give up the struggle.

"Be patient," advised Scalabrini. "Defend yourself; correct anything that may need correction, but stand firm! Do not, even for a fleeting moment, think of relinquishing your diocese! Not even if they told you the Pope wants it. It would be an unpardonable error." Bishop Bonomelli regained his courage.

This, in brief, is the story of many a year—and years, when difficult, pass slowly. In Rome it finally became clear that the Intransigents were demanding the head of this feared and steadfast opponent. To save him from the ire of his enemies it was decided to send him on a diplomatic mission to South America, without the need of having him resign from his diocese.

Again Bishop Scalabrini pleaded his cause. The length of Bonomelli's absence from Cremona was shortened by sending him to the Orient. This was a much shorter trip and led Bishop Bonomelli to write his well-known book, *An Autumn in the Orient*. On his return, again through Bishop Scalabrini, he made his peace with his bitterest adversary, the editor of the *Osservatore Cattolico*, Father Albertario!

It became very clear that Bishop Scalabrini, therefore, could hardly have acted as peacemaker between them unless he, himself, had not become reconciled with the editor.

In all probability someone in authority had gone to the fiery orator and writer from Lombardy and had made it clear that it was high time to rebuild the bridges that had been so woefully destroyed. Probably also time may have helped in making him see that "idealistic battles" are not won with diatribes and insults. In any case the editor of the *Osservatore Cattolico*, Father Albertario, must have at last become convinced that his adversaries had not only fought on the side of the Church, but, moreover, had used means that had been better and more far-reaching than his own. He had the civic and Christian courage to admit his error openly.

In 1894 Bishop Scalabrini went to Turin in Piedmont to take part in the Eucharistic Congress being held there. While in Turin he learned that Father Albertario was also there and had expressed the wish to apologize to him.

The Bishop gave his answer:

"Tell him that Bishop Scalabrini has forgotten everything, for he has never hated. He holds close to his heart, not as opponents, but as brothers, those who have offended him through error."

Encouraged by these words, Father Albertario presented himself before the bishop, knelt at his feet, and begged his pardon. The Servant of God lifted him to his feet and held him in a brotherly embrace. Two good men had made their peace, a peace which was never again broken.

Two years later the Opera dei Congressi met in general assembly in Piacenza. Father Albertario in his role as an exponent of the Catholic movement was asked to discuss one of the points on the agenda of the day. Bishop Scalabrini invited him to be his guest at his residence.

The newspapers of the day wrote that when the former reporter-priest took his place on the platform to address the audience, an intense murmur swept through the whole assembly. Too many knew all that had occurred between him and the bishop. And here he was speaking in the bishop's own house!

Father Albertario understood how impossible it was for him to turn the page as if nothing unpleasant had happened. He began with these words:

"There are people here today who no doubt are astonished at seeing me here in this house and in realizing that I have been allowed to speak to you. There is only one explanation for this—the greatness of Bishop Scalabrini's heart!"

After his talk a friend said to him:

"Bravo! Those words did you honor!"

"Bishop Scalabrini worked the miracle, and he will work many another," answered the priest.

A few years later, in May 1898, the revolutionary riots of Milan broke out and had to be suppressed by the police. The general in charge of the military government gave orders for the arrest of twenty-five newspaper reporters. Among them was Father Albertario.

The men were tried, found guilty, and sentenced to three years' imprisonment, plus a fine of 1,000 lire (about $200 at the time). Father Albertario was accused of "having lifted his voice against those who fired at the people begging for bread."

Bishop Scalabrini had been among those who had done their utmost to try to keep the priest from being brought to trial. When his efforts proved futile, he sought the King's pardon for him, and in the meantime he succeeded in lessening the hardships of the jail for the priest, obtaining permission for him to wear his priestly garb and to offer the holy sacrifice of the Mass.

The following May the political prisoners were granted a full pardon. No sooner did Father Albertario leave his prison than he hastened to write to his benefactor:

"My hands still bear the signs of my prison chains, but I cannot afford to lose a moment in fulfilling my duty toward Your Excellency. May God pour his blessings upon you and your diocese for the loving-kindness shown by you toward a suffering human being. . . .

"If ever the moment shall come when it may be granted to me to pay my homage to Your Excellency, I shall speak to you of certain matters, facts which I shall never reveal to anyone else. . . ."

We do not know whether that moment ever came, nor if those matters were ever revealed to the man who had been so bitterly attacked.

Father Albertario left his prison cell, shaken in health, and betook himself to his native village where he lived quietly until the day of his death, little more than three years later.

Thus ends the painful story of the relations between two courageous souls, two brave fighters both of them working for the same cause, though in different ways, the cause of the Church and the Pope. The same cause, and yet both finding the ground bitterly disputed by opposing battlelines!

Thus it ends, and ends well. The objective and documented exposition of facts does deplore and condemn a real and well-defined persecution unleashed against a venerable shepherd of the Church, guilty only in seeing things in different lights from his opponents. It establishes without error, where those really responsible for the deplorable conflict stood, pointing out clearly who was right and who was wrong. And the conclusion can be only one. The supernatural force springing forth from the Gospel of Christ, when it is truly alive and working, succeeds in conquering evil through virtue.

We have here a bishop accused, vilified, and injured in his dignity, his reputation, and in what a bishop holds most dear, love of the Church and devotion to the Vicar of Christ on earth. A bishop who, after undergoing all of this, opens his arms to those who have offended him, with no demands for satisfaction, no payment of damages.

Father Albertario also was great. In spite of his defects, he was a great standard-bearer, an aggressive one, daring, hated by some and idolized by others, obstinate and unwilling to surrender the banner he held. And yet one who, after having waved that same banner for almost thirty years in the face of his real and supposed enemies, lashing at them, annoying them, provoking and halting them in their tracks, lowers that banner before one of his most irreconcilable adversaries. Not only does he place that banner at his feet, but, recognizing the error of his ways, pronounces the words of sincere humility, the humility that exalts him who speaks them, "Forgive me, for I have sinned."

The quality of mercy in the bishop's heart pens a luminous page of exquisite evangelical virtue.

The spirit of humility in the reporter-priest who had been arrested and imprisoned, not because he was on the side of subversive elements, but because he had lined himself up with the hungry and the oppressed, lifts him in our estimation. As we look upon him, we cannot but feel that much will be forgiven him, for he loved much.

CHAPTER 15

The Good Helmsman

*The day when every family will come to kneel
at the feet of Mary . . . will see the
beginning of God's kingdom on earth . . .*

As EVERYONE KNOWS, the man with his hand steadily on the wheel and his eyes fixed on the path ahead of him, firm and strong no matter how rough the seas through which his ship is plowing, must be a good helmsman. Bishop Scalabrini was such a man. The struggles, the polemics, the difficulties he encountered from unworthy attacks and mortifying misunderstandings never for a single moment slowed up any of the activities he considered belonging to his pastoral life. In other words, in weather fair or foul he continued on his course without uncertainty or delay.

Let us take up once again where we left off. We should like to give all the facts of the situation, though we were almost anxious to make it as short as possible, for these facts pen a glorious page in the life of the bishop of Piacenza.

In his pastoral letters the bishop continued to face some of the most important problems of the moment. There was no occurrence or outstanding action upon which he did not comment in conformity with Catholic doctrine and the laws of the Catholic Church.

On July 13, 1881, a disgraceful incident took place in Rome. Few are ignorant of the attempt perpetrated by a mob of fanatical hoodlums to throw the venerated remains of Pope Pius IX into the Tiber River while they were being transported under cover of darkness from St. Peter's to the Basilica of St. Lawrence.

Bishop Scalabrini spoke of this outrage to his people of the diocese by commenting on the encyclical *Diuturnum*, and drawing from it inspiration for his flock, by urging them to show themselves as sincere Catholics, fearless in the face of attacks by the common enemy.

In 1882 a scandalous little sheet, *The Penitent*, made its appearance, and was published in Piacenza. It was dedicated to the spreading of atheism. The bishop struck out against it with so vigorous and lightninglike a move that *The Penitent* died as soon as it was born—without even a chance at making an act of contrition.

In 1884 the illness to which we have alluded previously forced the bishop to slow up on his pastoral visits. However, he kept on with the other activities of his ministry. In fact, in 1881 he came out with a strong comment on the papal document against Freemasonry, the encyclical *Humanum Genus*. In that year also he gave out new directives for Catholic action, the need of which seemed more pressing as time passed. He gave wise and pertinent counsel to labor associations, as he saw in this an efficacious means for lessening the influence of socialist propaganda among the workers. He encouraged the reform of sacred music in the same spirit which we find in later years in the *Motu Proprio* of St. Pius X. He spread devotion to the Blessed Virgin by encouraging the recitation of the rosary not only during the months dedicated to her but as a daily family practice.

He was the "man of the hour," a man of open mind toward all problems that were of interest to him or that worried him. Whether they were religious or civic, social or political, he never lost sight of the principal problem, the one he considered essential for others because it was essential for him. This was prayer, which, as he saw it, as he proved it, was the most powerful means for finding consolation, strength, and self-mortification. In a particular way he recommended prayer to Mary, as the source of life, hope, and fortitude for the world.

From prayer each day he drew inspiration, patience, courage, endurance, and even physical strength. The light which filtered faintly through the half-closed shutters of his private chapel was witness to his piety. The shepherd watched while his flock took what they considered to be a legitimate and necessary rest.

"The day when every family will come to kneel at the feet of Mary in filial devotion and humble confidence," he thought, "will see the beginning of the Kingdom of God on earth."

Again in 1884 two serious dangers delineated themselves on the horizon. One was moral: a bill aimed at legalizing divorce that was presented to the Chamber of Deputies. Bishop Scalabrini provoked a strong reaction against the bill among his people.

The second was physical. Cholera broke out in La Spezia. As he had done before, when epidemics had threatened, the bishop mobilized his clergy, organized service units, and declared himself ready to assist the stricken people. Luckily this time the epidemic was short-lived.

As always, he continued to point out that in any struggle against dangers which threatened either body or soul the most solid defense lay in the recitation of the rosary, and the most powerful helper was Mary, the Mother of Christ.

That same year saw the publication of the encyclical *Immortale Dei*, which dealt with the Christian concept of national life. This encyclical is one of the loftiest and most solemn ever to come from the brilliant pen of Leo XIII. The bishop of Piacenza was enthusiastic about it. He wrote to the Holy Father, expressing his satisfaction and his gratitude for the sublime concepts stated there and for the directives given. He immediately communicated it to his diocese, explaining it in detail, and advising the pastors to give special courses of instruction in it.

An auspicious date was fast approaching for the whole of

the Catholic world. In 1887 Leo XIII was to celebrate his golden jubilee as a priest. Bishop Scalabrini began preparing his flock for the celebration. In a letter to his diocese he exhorted them to see in the Pope, not the enemy of Italy as his enemies pointed him out to be, but a true friend. He compared him to the first great Leo, ever ready to unite himself with Italy in arresting the hordes of demagogic anarchy, thus saving the nation, as well as the inviolable seat of the Papacy, without spilling a drop of blood.

Furthermore, he organized public prayers in behalf of the Pope, organized the collection of Peter's pence, and made plans for the preparation of rich gifts to be presented to the Holy Father on the occasion of a diocesan pilgrimage from Piacenza to Rome. On the day appointed for the celebration of the jubilee he offered a solemn pontifical Mass in the cathedral. In his sermon he called for peace between the Papacy and Italy. His listeners enthusiastically agreed with him that this peace for the good of all concerned must be brought about with all possible speed.

In the first months of 1887 he indulged in one of those actions which seemed directed purposely toward drawing down upon him the ire of his enemies and the sympathy of his flock. But, as usual, he was only obeying the impulses of his own conscience.

A contingent of troops was leaving for Africa where Italy was fighting a war. They were boys under orders, boys who were fulfilling their duties to their motherland, boys who were obliged to fight, perhaps even to die. Bishop Scalabrini, certain that the conflict between the Italian Government and the Holy See could in no way prevent him from offering them the comfort of their religion, sent a short note to their commanding officer.

"The bishop of Piacenza," he wrote, "sends his blessings to the colonel and his men on their departure for Africa, begging God's blessing upon them and wishing them a safe going and a glorious return."

The colonel answered with a letter in which he thanked him for his words. The bishop had been the first to do this, but many others then followed his example. A storm of protest broke forth, but nothing came of it.

The year 1887 was marked by many sad events indeed. The region of Liguria was struck by a violent earthquake. The bishop was quick to launch a drive for funds in behalf of the stricken in the devastated zone, setting a personal example by giving much more than his scanty resources permitted. He had already proved his deep spirit of charity when he had aided the zones of northern Italy laid waste by a flood in 1882. In 1883 the little town of Casamicciola had been shattered by an earthquake and turned into a shambles. Then the bishop, in order to alleviate the sufferings of the homeless and starving people, had taken the pectoral cross sent to him as a gift by Pope Piux IX to a pawnshop —there to keep company with another precious object, the golden chalice which had procured him the needed funds with which to feed his poor of Piacenza, harassed by famine in 1879.

But the year 1887, so burdened with work and sad events, was not to end without one more sorrow with its consequent preoccupations being added to his own burdensome task.

On December 14 the celebrated "Forty Propositions" by Antonio Rosmini were placed on the Index.

The matter lay very close to the bishop's heart. As has already been said he was not a follower of Rosmini. Moreover, he had often given clear proof of his independence of thought from the Rosminian philosophy. The proof was self-evident by his having prescribed the teaching of the Thomistic philosophy in his seminaries and by promoting the publication of the *Divus Thomas* even before the encyclical *Aeterni Patris* had come out of Rome. But two hundred or so of his priests had studied Rosmini's theories, since these formed part of the legitimate studies at the seminaries. In his relations with these priests Bishop Scalabrini had to act with utmost prudence to prevent eventual defections. The latter might possibly come about because of the extreme confusion in the minds of many. What made the situation still more delicate was the fact that these priests were not "expendable men" but, for the most part, cultured and zealous, striving for the glory of God and the good of souls and devoted to their bishop as well as to the Holy See.

On this occasion, as on many others, Bishop Scalabrini penned a page which honors him as a man and as a bishop. In it he wisely brought into close harmony the rights which are the prerogative of authority and of freedom. With enlightened charity he lent himself not to break the bruised reed, nor to snuff out the sputtering candle flame, as is given in command by the Gospel. He had all those priests in the palm of his hand, for he held them all in his heart!

As far back as the year 1882, when a condemnation of Rosmini's writings was foreseen, he had written to his friend Bonomelli:

"I am not a Rosminian, yet now I do fear that condemnation with extreme anxiety. If it shall come, we are going to have many secret apostates and many public rebels. Among my priests I have about 200 who have studied Rosmini. I have been at pains during these years, in view of the condemnation that may come, to conquer their souls. While I have allowed them that freedom which the Church permits, I have sought to prepare them for that submission which the Pope may see fit to demand."

Rosmini's philosophy, made more appreciable by the holiness of Rosmini's life, was one of the debatable subjects. Zealous as the bishop was in upholding that true freedom of opinion, and respectful of the opinion of others, how could he have shown himself more strict than the Church who, in debatable matters, allows full freedom of thought or discussion? This is what his opponents wanted, but were they not narrow-minded? And, after all, what did it matter if they disapproved of his attitude, as long as it was fully justified and conformable with the dictates of conscience and it paved the way for an act of perfect charity?

Once he had written to the Jesuit, Father Cornoldi, the statement which follows:

"I was, am, and always shall be firm in defending that honest freedom of discussion which the Church permits in debatable matters. However, I have been, am, and ever shall be, with God's help, just as firm in demanding that my priests bow in full and perfect submission to the decrees of the Holy See."

And thus it was, but the results he achieved were principally due to the spirit of kindliness he used along with his firmness, results which meant complete success on his part.

He made the decree of condemnation known to his clergy and accompanied it with a comprehensive, dignified, and prudent letter in which he pointed out that it would be a most foolish mistake on the part of Rosmini's adversaries to boast of having achieved a triumph. The triumph was not theirs. It was a triumph for truth, and hence it belonged to Christ Himself who is especially triumphant when everyone bows in obedience to Him. He pointed out, moreover, that those who had followed the doctrine of Rosmini should not feel disheartened. True they had followed his doctrine, thinking it was in conjunction with truth, yet they had been ready even before the condemnation to renounce it whenever the Church should have decided to condemn it. Everyone had reason for rejoicing, he added. The former, as they had the assurance of being in the right, the latter because they had been saved from the danger of falling into error.

His words went straight to the heart of his priests, who well knew the loftiness of spirit of the man who had written them.

How well they remembered the day when several of them had been accused before the Holy See on a matter of doctrine! In the Servant of God they had found a champion who had spoken these words in their defense to the Holy Father:

"Holy Father, am I therefore forced to say, as St. Ambrose affirms, that false witnesses dare at times to reach even to the throne of Peter and find credit there?"

And when it seemed to him that Leo XIII was not as yet fully persuaded as to the justice of his defense, he had added:

"Your Holiness, when a bishop is not believed in matters such as these, he can do naught else except lay his miter at the feet of the Pope, and this I am ready to do even at this very moment."

Faced with such adamantine strength, the Holy Father had not insisted further.

Would they now make of their defender "a liar"?

Not one of his priests failed to submit himself to the paternal exhortation of his bishop, humbly and completely. Not a single one assumed an attitude which might be considered as lacking in discipline. The Pope was deeply moved when informed of what had taken place and declared that he wished to show his deep satisfaction to the bishop.

In consequence, sincere in his belief that his method had been proved right by the ready response he received, he continued to hold his Rosminian priests in high esteem. Although warning them with that pastoral authority which distinguished him, that the "Forty Propositions of Rosmini" were for students and sympathizers of the Rosmini doctrine as "forty rocks to be steered clear of," he never failed to work closely with them and to promote them, proud and happy that their act of obedience had offered the saintly priest of Rovereto the kind of homage he would have most desired. Moreover, had they not given everyone a perfect example by that same obedience?

CHAPTER 16

Roses and Thorns

. . . say to the Holy Father that
we will judge as he judges,
work as he works . . .

THE ITALIAN GOVERNMENT was entirely under the thumb of the Freemasons, a fact caused by the forced absence of militant Catholics from the political life of the country. As a result, the Masons kept on showing greater and greater effrontery in their plans against the Church by launching law after law aimed at harming the clergy. In the meantime, in Campo dei Fiori, one of the squares of Rome, a monument to Giordano Bruno was being erected, as an anti-altar to the Vatican.

Bishop Scalabrini became more and more firmly convinced that the most urgent need of the moment and the most profitable lay in strengthening the tree at its very roots. In 1889 he set about making preparations for a national catechetical convention. It was the first of its kind. Ten cardinals, twenty-five archbishops, and eighty-four bishops accepted the plan. Alfonso Cardinal Capecelatro was chosen president.

At the convention, the problems inherent to the teaching of catechism were fully and profoundly discussed. The first problem dealt with the compilation of a single text for the whole of Italy. Particular attention was given to religious schools, and it was unanimously agreed that immediate steps should be taken. Through the authoritative interest of the bishop the teaching of the catechism was to be based strictly on Christology. This is the very method which fifty years later was so enthusiastically and so authoritatively upheld as the most appropriate and effective. The Pope gave his approval and his blessing with a brief.

At the concluding session of the convention Bishop Scalabrini, addressing Alfonso Cardinal Capecelatro, the president, reporting to the Holy Father on the work done, said these words:

". . . say to the Holy Father that we shall ever be proud to think as he thinks in all things, to judge as he judges, to feel as he feels, to work as he works, to suffer with him, to battle with him and for him. . . ."

In October, weakened in health by the efforts put forth for the success of the convention, and for other reasons, Bishop Scalabrini fell ill with typhoid fever. Bishop Bonomelli also fell ill at the same time, but before the end of the year both were well on the road to recovery. They congratulated each other by agreeing that after all "it is asinine to die because of other people's faults," and that the only way to keep on living for the salvation of souls is "to let God provide and to keep on doing as much good as possible."

Between 1889 and 1891 the bishop made a third pastoral visit, although he had been advised to allow his assistants to take up part of it. The direct contact with his flock was a satisfaction which he could not easily renounce.

During all these years the bishop had dedicated himself intensively to a beneficent work, of which we shall speak more extensively later. Hence he lacked the time he needed for writing his usual elaborate pastoral letters which were real treatises and which aroused such great interest even beyond his own diocese. However, there is no dearth of "episcopal acts," among which we find that of 1891, dealing with what has become known as the "Magna Carta of the Labor

Movement," the famous encyclical of Pope Leo XIII, *Rerum Novarum.*

Later he dedicated long hours of study to this encyclical, and wrote on it at length. He showed in these writings his profound knowledge of social problems and his deep sympathy for the laboring classes. His writings on this question were later published under the title *Socialism and the Action of the Clergy.*

Another of the "acts" dealt with the third centenary of the death of St. Aloysius which was being celebrated that year. In it the bishop presented St. Aloysius as the champion of purity. Having brought into focus the central Christian value of purity, he urged the faithful to rediscover the meaning and power of it to the contemporary world through living example.

Between 1891 and 1892 he reduced the number of parishes in his diocese, overcoming rather heavy opposition. He gave special attention to the celebration of the fourth centenary of the discovery of America, and promoted the Society of Adoration for Prayers of Reparation Among Catholic Nations. He considered this the best means for calling the people of the world together before the Eucharistic throne at a time when it appeared as if everything were conspiring to draw minds and hearts from Our Lord Jesus Christ.

A man of broad vision and initiative, he turned his thoughts and his actions continuously to the Source whence any initiative draws substance and significance. He never lost the occasion to point out this Source to his children with the love of a father who longed to see them draw from it ever more abundant grace.

In 1893 he founded the Sodality of St. Opilio for the benefit of poor seminarians, and he gave vigorous impetus to the Sodality for the Promotion of Vocations, that there might never be a dearth of priests in the diocese.

It can be said that his efforts in good and worthy causes never ended.

Among his successes in Piacenza was a model recreation center for boys. Suddenly there appeared on the scene in an anonymous guise an illustrious promoter of a Lay Community House. Advertisements in the daily papers gave the purpose of the project "as a desire for drawing young people away from the dangers lurking in the streets, and giving them rest and recreation from the hardships of school and of work, as well as upholding their moral and civic education." It was clearly an attempt at counteracting the bishop's initiative, which had met so favorable a reaction from the general public. It was clear also that Bishop Scalabrini would in no way ignore the challenge and keep silent. In fact, in a letter written to all the pastors in his diocese he hastened to explain what in general were the goals of such institutions as suggested and willed by the Freemasons. He never for a single moment, however, went into a discussion of the promoter of the new project.

A polemic immediately ensued. Meetings were called. But due to the timely intervention of the bishop, the project failed and not a word more was heard about it.

Worldly successes had little effect in giving the bishop any great feeling of pleasure. He was pleased only for the sake of that amount of prestige which they might give to the bishop, to the "pastoral torch" destined to burn bright and in full view in the Church. As far as he was concerned, he preferred to accept those afflictions with which, as he well knew and often repeated, God enriches those whom he loves. As we have had occasion to see, and as we shall see again, these afflictions were never absent.

The year 1895 marked the completion of his first twenty years as bishop of Piacenza. The diocese decided to take advantage of the occasion to gather around him in ever-increasing devotion. His sorrows had made him ever more deserving of its veneration.

On the day set aside for the celebration a precious miter was offered by the people of Piacenza to their beloved bishop. It was accompanied by an album containing thousands upon thousands of signatures. The heart of the shepherd was filled with joy at the loving tribute of his flock.

CHAPTER 17

Advanced Post

. . . time to stand up and be counted
ready for any eventuality to hold
on to the Faith . . .

THE MANY preoccupations and sufferings which had been his had undermined the bishop's health already weakened by his former illness, but they had not succeeded in slowing up his pastoral activities. The bishop continued to concentrate his efforts in solving problems which even today are still of vital importance. His work and his methods make us easily appreciate his feeling for the *modern* in the best sense of the word. We realize, the more we read and the more we learn about him, that he was farseeing as shepherd of souls and clear-sighted as leader of men.

The problems which he tackled with that decisive action so characteristic of him were: Catholic action, the press, and economic-social action.

In Catholic action he was always a deep believer and worker ever since the days when he was pastor. As a bishop he had promoted it from the first day of his episcopate, as we have seen. But events were following one upon the other in ever increasing rhythm. While on one side a greater and more considerable number of the "faithful" were deserting the fold and denying their faith, on the other side, those who remained grew cold and slothful in the traditional practices of the Church. These last seemed unwilling to lift as much as a little finger to sweep back the flood or stem the tide of evil which was about to engulf them. While the enemy acted without letup and won ever new positions, many, too many, Catholics watched with idle hands and even drew back into the shadows, fearful of the storm, the rumblings of which grew louder each day and filled them with terror.

If this situation had gone on, the army of Christ would have been reduced to a band of sleepwalkers in a boundless desert.

A shepherd in the full knowledge of his duty to his flock could not allow the possibility of the wolf coming to find that flock asleep and helpless. He could not permit this, because Christ came to this earth to bring fire, not smoking embers. And because the Prince of Peace also did not fail to speak the warning that in certain circumstances he who has two garments is obliged to sell one of them in order to procure a sword.

In the year 1896 Bishop Scalabrini wrote a fiery pastoral letter in which he showed how Catholic action is an urgent necessity. He defined it as the way and the means for bringing Christ back into the school, the habits of the people, the family, the society. Politics, he stated, had its place in the life of man, but was not to be made use of as was done by the enemies of the Church. Catholic action could bring about a moral and civic regeneration which could naturally improve the political life of the country.

He quoted from the Pope's own words:

"With conditions such as they are at present, it is incumbent upon Italian Catholics to stand up and be counted, ready to face any eventuality and bear any trial in order to hold on to the inestimable gift of faith. Today there can only be room for two camps, both with clearly defined boundaries, the Catholic camp with men and women in it who are resolute in their intention to be always and forever united with their bishops and their Pope, and the enemy camp which is opposing them. Those who through cowardice and lukewarmness fear to show themselves as Catholics and love to take the middle of the road (could these be the 'liberal' Catholics of today?) by this very action are helping to swell the enemy's numbers.

"Now that everything conspires to the detriment of religion and the Church," the bishop went on, quoting from the Pope, "it would be useless to try to stem the evil that is threatening to overpower us, unless those who have Catholic interests at heart do not close their ranks and clasp hands in understanding and lofty purpose . . .

"It is not enough, to stand on the defensive against Freemasonry (the dreaded enemy of those days), but it is pertinent for Catholics to come out into the battlefield and give challenge. This cannot be done unless the enemy is opposed, written word by written word, teaching by teaching, school of thought by school of thought, association by association, convention by convention, action by action, strong and militant. . . .

"Hence," concluded the bishop, "local committees of Catholic action must be established without further delay in each parish of the diocese, and they must, moreover, once they are established, be maintained, and maintained vigorous and hard-working.

"My word this time," he added as an afterthought, "is not a word said in exhortation, but in command. And I am directing it principally to you, my venerable and worthy co-workers in the salvation of souls. . . ."

But Bishop Scalabrini was not satisfied with giving orders. He himself set the example by becoming an organizer. In a short time the parish committees of Catholic action in the diocese rose to 180, without counting the youth sections, the labor groups, etc.

At the same time he faced the problem of the press, the "weapon that thunders out more widely and has a far longer range than the cannon."

Well do we know what is meant by what the press says in the service of an idea. Well do we know what it has done and well do we see what it is doing, whether good or evil, since it is a double-edged sword. Well do we realize that in battling against a newspaper there is a great difference between having one's own to pit against the opposition and not having one at all.

In Piacenza the enemies against religion and against the Church had at their disposal not just one, but a number of papers, while the one Catholic organ, *L'Amico del Popolo,* came out only once every two weeks.

Bishop Scalabrini did not rest until he had made it a daily paper, paying no attention to the necessary sacrifices. A daily paper, even in those days, was an expensive proposition, yet he succeeded. Upheld as he was by the Catholic organizations, and making himself their loud-speaker as it were, and their defender, beneficial effects were soon evident. These were the benefits which the bishop had promised himself to achieve in the cause of truth and of the Catholic faith.

But in 1898 the reactionary storm which had broken out also against Catholic associations in all of Italy seemed to be overwhelming everything in its path, even hope of success.

The working masses, exasperated by exploitation and by poverty and instigated by socialist agitators, were showing more and more evident signs of unrest. Then came the announcement of the increase of the price of bread.

It was the well-known straw that broke the camel's back. Violent outbreaks occurred, first in the region of Romagna and in Emilia, then in Le Marche, in Tuscany, and in the region around Naples and in Sicily. They had their climax in the bloody riots of Milan.

In Piacenza the movement began on May 1, a day dedicated to labor. Results were serious—one dead and several wounded.

Bishop Scalabrini had always been on the side of the people. This attitude was not demagogy on his part, but stemmed from his desire to see the worker treated justly. When Leo XIII had issued his famous encyclical *Rerum Novarum,* he had greeted with exultation the placing of Christ into the problem of "social justice." He saw in this the means for its solution and for the establishment of that new order in conformity with evangelical principles.

Deeply hurt at what had taken place, he first of all provided for the families of the victims of the riots. Then he proceeded to plead with the authorities, both local and national, to take the needed steps that would tend toward soothing troubled spirits, rather than embitter them still further. To all he directed a letter exhorting calm and mutual understanding.

Within himself, however, an idea was taking root. Was not the time ripe for striking at the causes of the evil and thus cure the evil, rather than to make use of violent repressions or of exhortations for calm? Since sacrosanct rights were being denied or trampled upon, why not make up his mind to induce the ones responsible for this situation, to respect and guarantee the rights of others? Why leave the defense of the poor and of the laboring classes to those who denied God and fought the Christian religion? Had not Christ Himself first given to them the joyful tidings? Was it not His Church who, in His name, declared it a sin crying to God for vengeance to oppress the poor and defraud the laborer of his just wage?

Action followed thought. The bishop published a pamphlet called *Socialism and the Action of the Clergy.* In it he made his own the concepts expressed by Leo XIII in his encyclical. The duties of capital as well as those of labor

were brought out clearly and distinctly. He pointed out how
the Church had the absolute right not only to solve the "social question" on the basis of distributive justice, but also
with regard to liberty, property, and family. This was contrary to materialistic socialism.

In 1890 the horizon began to clear. The government
which had dissolved all Catholic societies on a par with subversive ones was now showing signs of a milder attitude.

Part of the merit for this should be attributed to Bishop
Scalabrini, who had discussed the problem in question
authoritatively, even going as high as the head of the government himself. With matters settled, the bishop lost no time.
He set about gathering together his lost and dispersed flock,
reconstituted the parish committees which had been dis-
banded, and in a short time he reorganized his army of Catholic actionists, inspiring them to work for religion, for the
Church, and for the people.

The twentieth century was just dawning, the century of
the Blessed Sacrament. The Servant of God willed to dedicate it to the Holy Eucharist.

Again, as always, he drew his strength, light, patience, and
charity from his divine Lord in the Holy Eucharist. In the
most difficult moments of his life, whenever he had to make
grave decisions, he withdrew to the chapel. There he begged
the Divine Counselor to make him see clearly and act justly.
On his leaving the chapel, he appeared resolute, sure of
himself, almost as though the decisions to be made or the
answers to be given had been written for him on a screen and
in definite terms. At times it seemed as though many things
were crumbling around him. Now and again his reputation
and his bishop's chair seemed to totter. But he fearlessly
continued onward, steadfast and true, not only unconquered
but unconquerable.

Hence, whenever he spoke of Jesus and His presence in the

Blessed Sacrament, especially to his priests and his seminarians, he looked as though he were transfigured.

His great wish, what he strove after with all his soul and sustained with his consecrated hands, was to see Christ in the Blessed Sacrament become the very life of the new century, even from its beginning.

Toward this goal he worked unceasingly. He willed that devotion to the Holy Eucharist be treated in all its aspects in sermons and in writing. The Church has always considered this devotion principally and eminently one to be fostered by its priests. Bishop Scalabrini pointed out how necessary it was for a priest to lead a eucharistic life and diffuse it among the faithful in his care. Thus he gave substance and form to a real and distinct diocesan eucharistic code.

As has been said many times, this Servant of God was a man of exceptional character. He saw everything and he was interested in anything that might fulfill his burning desire to give glory to God in every possible manner.

The Cathedral of Piacenza, erected by Bishop Aldo at the beginning of the twelfth century, had suffered through the years. The beauty of the building had been marred and restorations were needed.

The task called for work of colossal proportions and a large sum of money.

"But," said the bishop, "the cathedral is, after all, the house of God, the home of all. It is the compendium of civic life, so much so in fact that under its arches and among its columns, as in the arms of a mother, we all feel ourselves to be brothers."

So he asked his flock to demonstrate their attachment to their city and their faith by contributing generously.

This time also disappointments were not lacking, nor trials, nor the ridicule of his enemies. The latter even went so far as to define his proposal as a ridiculous piece of business, *fin de siècle*. In spite of everything, however, the dawn of the twentieth century was a witness to the joy of the people of Piacenza when they saw their great temple restored almost completely to its pristine splendor. Almost a half million lire was spent on the project, a sum which in those years was fabulous.

In 1901 the cathedral was reopened to the public. The bishop, promoter of the project, its very soul as it were, celebrated the solemn rite of his episcopal jubilee. It was a happy day for Piacenza. Its echo was felt throughout Italy and even beyond.

Twenty-five years as a bishop always represents a complexity of work and outstanding achievements, worthy of recognition and gratitude. The twenty-five years lived by Bishop Scalabrini were remarkable for duties fulfilled with unflagging zeal and ingenuity. In addition they stood out because of the strenuous struggles he coped with, and because of his providential and stouthearted attitude in the delicate situation between Church and State in Italy which was brought about by the loss of the temporal power.

It should be stated here that the first one to render homage to his person, but perhaps even more to his multiform, complex and even daring work as shepherd of his flock, was Leo XIII. The Pope addressed to him a most pertinent brief. After recalling to him how throughout the years he had always given him so many proofs of his filial devotion, the Holy Father added how joyful he should be in the celebration of his jubilee as bishop. He concluded by saying that notwithstanding the fact that sufferings and hardships had been his, he had brought about copious good fruit.

Many important Roman prelates, men whose names have been written in gold in the history of the Church, as well as others from all of Italy and not a few from foreign lands, the archbishop of New York among them, paid him homage for his wisdom, zeal, and spirit of charity.

Nor did the city administration of his own Piacenza forget him. The recognition was unanimous for this adopted son. The Como diocese felt proud of having given so great a "son" to Piacenza.

A group of illustrious Italian women offered him vestments, richly embroidered in silk and gold. At the head of this group was the Queen Mother, Margherita of Savoy.

A gem-studded golden chalice was offered to him. Bishop Bruni of Modena, who had initiated the idea for the offering, wrote on this occasion:

"I know that the illustrious prelate of Piacenza in the difficult days of his ministry, which were far from few, while celebrating the Mass, kept repeating: 'Bitter is my cup, O Lord, but I will drink it willingly for the sake of my love for Thee and for my children's sake.' How fitting it would be if on the occasion of his jubilee his people could say to him: 'Father, you offered the chalice of your sufferings to God for us. Accept now from us in thanksgiving this chalice of joy and exultation.' "

The people of Piacenza had answered the appeal with enthusiasm and generosity. No one was ignorant of the holy intentions that had always inspired the bishop in his acceptance of God's will! On the day of his jubilee, Bishop Scalabrini was truly able to offer his Eternal Father the holy sacrifice of the Mass in the chalice of joy and exultation.

The cathedral was jammed with people. Even the civic authorities were all present. One of the daily papers spoke of the kindly, illustrious, and charitable Bishop Scalabrini and pointed out as truly a "miracle," the feeling of peace and undertanding which had been created and admitted "how good it is to get together as friends."

In these happy circumstances the good shepherd did not forget his favorite children—the needy, the old people, and the unfortunate.

The great heart of this servant of God was always most

sensitive to any form of misfortune. Even as a child he used for the needy the allowance of money given him by his mother that he might buy something to eat with his bread. He often had exchanged the white bread in his lunch for the black bread of his less fortunate small friends.

We have seen how, as a bishop, he made his charity heroic, that it might not be simply a useless gesture. But the thought of his "dear needy," as he always called them, was with him night and day. He gave to them all he had as long as he had anything.

A daily paper in Piacenza had once published a humorous cartoon where the bishop was represented in the act of feeding the roosters and chickens in a barnyard. Each bird showed the face of one of the many exponents of the anti-clerical party.

It was the simple truth. Bishop Scalabrini was known to be most generous with those who did him harm, or attempted to do him harm.

He often visited the prisoners in their cells, bringing them food and gifts. Perhaps more important than these was the priceless gift of his fatherly presence, his fatherly understanding and love. Two episodes which occurred during his visits are worthy of note.

Because of the riots of 1898, a certain socialist lawyer had been jailed. When he heard that the bishop was coming to see him he said:

"If he dares to put his foot within my cell, I swear that he will leave it with a broken head."

The bishop did not allow himself to be frightened. He entered the cell and remained talking with the prisoner for a long time. On his leaving, he exclaimed:

"God is indeed merciful!"

On another occasion, when he had gone to the prison to distribute the Easter Communion to the unfortunate inmates, a moving incident took place. While he was distributing Holy Communion, one of the men kneeling at the railing held his arm and, gazing at the Sacred Host, exclaimed:

"Lord, Thou knowest that I am innocent."

A short time passed. A review of the trial of the man involved was initiated and he was proved innocent. The bishop had not only been deeply touched but had acted effectively in his paternal charity.

The celebration of his jubilee would not have been complete if he had not remembered those of his children who were in need. He set aside a sum of money to be distributed to the needy and the afflicted, in the payment of debts, in assisting the sick, and in feeding the aged and those in prison. The prisoners who had known his generosity sent him the following message of devotion and good wishes:

"God will not deny us what we ask Him, for Your Excellency, you who have always been a father to the unfortunate, who have always consoled the afflicted. It is a great consolation for those within these walls to think that someone pities them and prays for them!"

Almost as if to gather together all these spiritual harmonies, and to celebrate them appropriately, Maestro Perosi, the great composer of sacred music, gave his oratorio entitled *Christmas* in the Municipal Theater. It was as a homage of music and art to the mutual understanding of men who had found themselves brothers before God, in an outburst of good will toward one another.

CHAPTER 18

Far Beyond His Flock

. . . and other sheep have I also . . .

THE JUBILEE CELEBRATIONS took place in June 1901. One
month later, still weary from the joyful yet fatiguing experience, Bishop Scalabrini, who was then sixty-two years
of age, sailed from Genoa for North America.

Here, however, before we speak of his voyage, we must
remind the reader that he is still far from knowing the complete Scalabrini. He has become acquainted with an intelligent, virtuous youth, an upright, zealous, dynamic priest, a
model pastor. He has learned of him as a wise and saintly
bishop, tireless and courageous, one whose pastoral work
would have been sufficient to fill a whole lifetime and make
it worthy of admiration. But he has not as yet been informed
about the greatest of his achievements. So far we have made
no mention of it, that we might give it the place, the impact,
and the importance it so well deserves. This is his work as a
pioneer in the interest of the Italian emigrants.

In order to show this work in its completeness, that is
from the moment of its inception to its full maturity, it is
necessary to go back several years and cover step by step the
whole long, difficult road. We cannot, on the other hand,
keep from stating now that this form of apostolate, which
as a general rule is not part of the normal duties of the episcopate, leads us to consider two factors. The manner in
which the bishop conceived this work, the ways he used to
make it known, induce us not so much to stand in admira-

John Baptist Scalabrini receiving the blessing of St. Pius X before leaving for a visit to his American missionaries and immigrants.

Bishop Scalabrini with President Theodore Roosevelt, the White House, October 10, 1901.

. . . Blessing the corner stone of the Church of St. Mary of Mount Carmel, Utica, New York, September 15, 1901.

. . . Off to South America, June 17, 1904.

The bishop among his missionaries in Brazil, 1904. On his right is Father Massimo Rinaldi, later Bishop of Rieti, Italy.

. . . Lying in state, June 1, 1905.

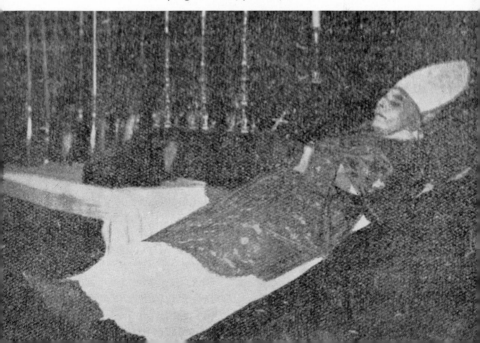

Tomb of John Baptist Scalabrini in the Cathedral of Piacenza, Italy.

Bishops present at the removal of Bishop Scalabrini's body from the public cemetery to the Cathedral of Piacenza. (1) Archbishop James Della Chiesa, later Pope Benedict XV; (2) Bishop Jeremias Bonomelli of Cremona; (3) Bishop John Baptist Nasalli Rocca, later Cardinal Archbishop of Bologna.

Monument to Bishop Scalabrini at Bassano del Grappa, Italy. The flags represent each nation in which his missionaries are now working.

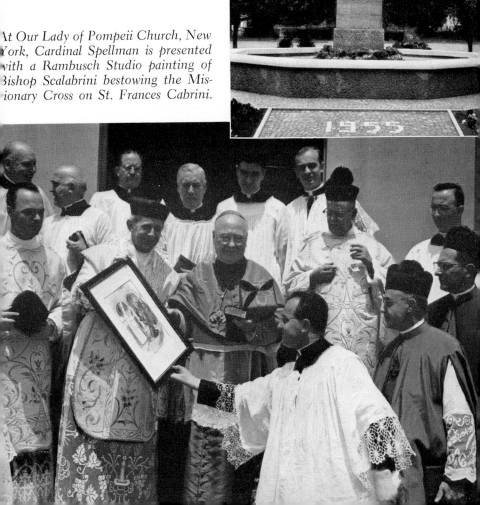

At Our Lady of Pompeii Church, New York, Cardinal Spellman is presented with a Rambusch Studio painting of Bishop Scalabrini bestowing the Missionary Cross on St. Frances Cabrini.

Archbishop Richard Cushing with the Scalabrinian Fathers at Boston before delivering a commemorative address on Bishop Scalabrini, June 30, 1955.

James Cardinal Lercaro evokes the memory of Bishop Scalabrini to a vast throng in the Cathedral of Piacenza, Italy, June 1, 1955.

Patrick Cardinal Hayes blesses Our Lady of Pompeii Church, New York. On his right is Rev. A. Demo, P.S.S.C.; on the far left, Rev. Joseph Pernicone, now Auxiliary Bishop of New York.

Adeodato Cardinal Piazza, Secretary of the Consistorial Congregation, with Samuel Cardinal Stritch of Chicago blesses the aged, Villa Scalabrini, North Lake City, Ill.

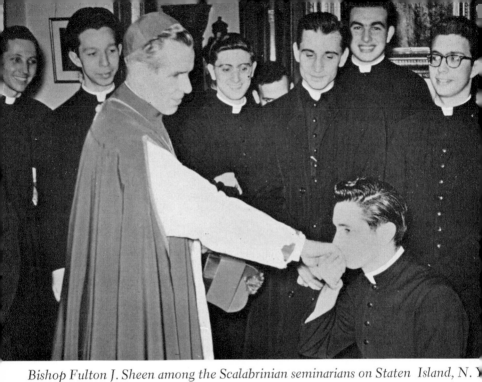

Bishop Fulton J. Sheen among the Scalabrinian seminarians on Staten Island, N. Y.

John O. Pastore, of Rhode Island, first Italo-American governor and U. S. senator
among Scalabrinian Fathers and students.

Pius XII *presents the Scalabrinian Fathers with a replica of Our Lady of Loreto as a pilgrim statue for the Italian communities in France.*

The world-famous "Schola Cantorum" of the Sistine Chapel, directed by Maestro Lorenzo Perosi, pays tribute to Our Lady on her departure to France.

The statue of Our Lady carried through St. Peter's Square by Italian migrants.

The statue is flown to France in the private plane of Italy's president.

. . . Carried
into the Basilica
of Notre Dame,
Paris.

Scalabrinian Fathers at
the exit of a mine where
they visited Italian immigrant miners in Belgium.

Father R. Lombardi, S.J., famous Italian author visits Italian immigrants in Belgium.

Italian immigrants on pilgri to the Marian Shrine of Einsiedeln, Switzerland.

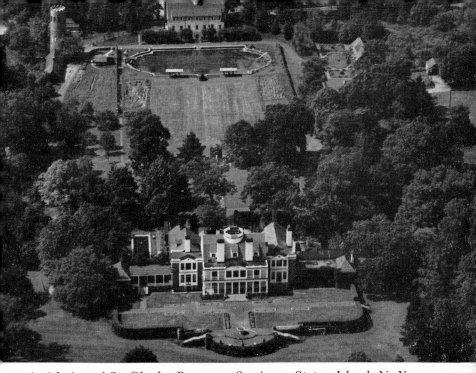

Aerial view of St. Charles Borromeo Seminary, Staten Island, N. Y.

Seminary in Bassano del Grappa, Italy, dedicated to Bishop Scalabrini in 1930, on the 25th anniversary of his death.

Villa Scalabrini, home for the Italian aged, North Lake City, Illinois.

St. Rocco's Church, Thornton, Rhode Island.

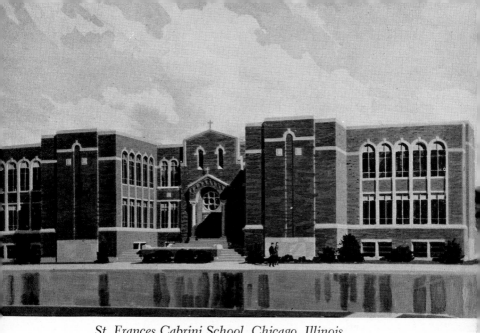

St. Frances Cabrini School, Chicago, Illinois.

Shrine to Our Lady Queen of Peace in São Paulo, Brazil.

Our Lady of All So[u]l[s]
Church, Hamilton, [On]
tario, Canada.

Immaculate Concept[ion]
Church,   Unande[ra]
N.S.W., Australia.

tion of the prodigious energy of his genius, but rather to consider the yearning that moved him. This was the typical yearning of a shepherd of souls, intimately united to the Eternal Shepherd, as the branch is to the tree. This was the yearning of him who, although appointed to the guardianship of a definite flock, did not neglect thinking of all those who were invoking help and salvation.

The Divine Master Himself has said: "And other sheep have I also who are not of this flock. They also must I seek that there may be but one flock and one Shepherd."

In these words of Our Lord Bishop Scalabrini saw a new problem before him. He knew he had been given another task, one that he could not refuse, without falling short of the call that made of him a successor of the Apostles and a pillar of the Church.

Now let us return to the first years in the episcopate of Bishop Scalabrini, more exactly perhaps to the time of his first pastoral visit. It was then he had his initial intimate talks with the humblest of his people, the aged, men and women, whom he was wont to question about the number in their family, their work, and where their sons and daughters lived. Frequently he heard that a son or other member of the family was away, far away—in the Americas. There they had gone to seek for the bread that was not abundant at home.

At the end of his pastoral visit he added the numbers together. Twenty-eight thousand of his people had left Italy because of lack of work. Fathers and sons lived far from their native land, far from their families, far from the spiritual ties of their own parish, abandoned in strange lands, among people indifferent to them and often hostile.

The picture was a sad one, both to the eyes of the man and the Italian. It appeared sadder still to the eyes of the bishop. His heart was very heavy. And yet the picture before his eyes was only a small detail of a far larger picture, a far sadder one!

Italy with thirty million inhabitants at that time had 900,000 of its people outside its borders. A multitude indeed. All of them, more or less, were in the same tragic condition. They could have been called "pariahs," forced to earn their bread for a heavy price, namely, the giving up of what a man holds dearest on earth, his religion, his country, his family. While in other countries the national government did at least a little for the emigrants, to make them feel that the mother country still considered them her children, branches still united to the great family tree, the Italian authorities watched powerless as Italy's sons left her shores, unable to keep up any kind of helpful contact with them.

It has already been said, and more than once, that when Bishop Scalabrini set his mind upon something that meant a charitable duty, or a problem of the apostolate, he did not rest until he had done all that was possible with the means he had at hand.

Face to face with the emigration problem, once he had seen it with his own eyes and taken it deep into his own heart, he made up his mind to do something about it. It tormented his very soul. The missionary vocation which had beckoned to him so strongly as a youth was alive once more.

The problem of emigration and the migratory phenomenon had to be observed and studied at their very roots, as to their causes, their character, and their consequences. Bishop Scalabrini dedicated himself wholly and zealously to his task as a student of social questions. The more he studied the problems involved, the more he became convinced that he had to find a concrete solution. The decisive action by which he ordered his thoughts and brought them to a measure of success occurred through an incident which he himself tells about in his first booklet on the problem.

"As I was walking through the railroad station in Milan," he writes, "I saw the vast waiting room, the side aisles, and the adjacent square invaded by a large mass of people. They were poorly dressed, miserable, and huddled into groups. Their faces, burned brown by the sun, were worn and etched with the deep wrinkles of hard years of toil at home and in the fields. In their eyes transpired the tumult of emotions tearing at their hearts. There were old men, their backs bent by age and hardships, men in the flower of their youth, women with babies in their arms, young children clinging to their mother's skirts, young boys and girls in their teens. All of them shared only one thought. They had become brothers in a common tragedy and in a common goal.

"They were the emigrants. They belonged to the various regions of northern Italy and they were all awaiting the train that would take them to the shores of the Mediterranean, whence they would sail for the distant Americas, North or South. There they hoped to find a fate a little less adverse, a land a little less ungrateful to their sweat.

"They were set and ready to go, some sent for by relatives who had preceded them in the voluntary exodus, others not knowing exactly where they were bound, but every one of them attracted there by that tremendous urge to migrate, such as even birds experience. So many times they had heard the oft-repeated cry that in America there was work, well-rewarded work. All you needed were brawny arms and a firm will.

"Their native village had been left behind, not without tears. So many memories linked them to their past. And yet without regret they were ready to abandon the fatherland. Did they not know it only under the two odious forms of the draft and the tax collector? For the evicted, the penniless, and the hungry, the land that provides bread for their family is their land. Far away was a land where they hoped to find bread, less scarce at least, although the work and the sweat might be as great.

"I left the station shaken with pity. A fit of racking sadness surged through my heart. What an accumulation of sorrows and privations must have occurred to make this painful step seem a sweet one! How many disillusions, how many new sorrows would the uncertain future have in store for them? How many would emerge victorious from the tremendous struggles which lay ahead for mere existence? How many would succumb, helpless in the face of the storm? How many, after having found food for their bodies, would lose the food necessary for their souls? How many in a wholly material struggle would forget the faith of their fathers?

"From that day onward my mind often went back to those poor unfortunates. And the scene I witnessed at the Milan Station recalls another one to me, one not less heartbreaking. I have never seen it, but I have read of it between the lines in letters written by friends. I have pictured it from tales told to me by men who have traveled a great deal. I see all those poor miserable creatures landing in a strange country. The people they meet speak a language they cannot understand, and unfortunately among these strangers are some who take advantage of them. Often they fall victims to empty, golden promises. Alone, broken in body and spirit, many succumb under the burden. There are those who are successful, but among these too many of them have lost both faith and morals.

"Confronted with such a state of affairs, I have asked myself again and again what was to be done to cure the evil. Now and again I happened to read in the daily press some government pronouncement. These put the authorities and the public on guard against a certain type of speculators, veritable slave traders, blind to everything except their thirst for gold, who lure their poor victims away from their native land with bribes and false promises. When I learn in letters from friends of mine that these speculators, these vilest of men, are Italians, when I learn that the exploiters of the Italian immigrants in America are of Italian blood, when I am told that these men, if such they can be called, hold their brothers in almost abject slavery and their own native land is deaf to their pleas, blind to their abandonment, then the blush of shame rises to my cheeks. Then I feel myself humiliated as a priest and as an Italian, and again I wonder how I can be of help to them."

With so clear and realistic a vision of the problem in its diverse aspects, that is, human, civic, social, and religious, certainly not a partial but a comprehensive one, Bishop Scalabrini decided to call the attention of the Italian clergy and the Italian people to the whole shameful situation. These are some of his words:

"Let us join together in charity, because charity is God's own messenger at the peace table and knows no party. The blood of Christ brings us all together as brothers into one faith and one hope and renders all debtors to all."

Before publishing his appeal, a veritable trumpet call to a holy war, he had sketched out a "plan," as it were, and submitted it to John Cardinal Simeoni, prefect of the Sacred Congregation for the Propagation of Faith. On February 3, 1887, he received the prefect's answer. The cardinal informed him that his letter had been received. Moreover, he told Bishop Scalabrini that the possibility for the appointment of a committee to study the Italian emigration problem was being considered. The committee would look after the religious and temporal interests of the Italian emigrants. In conclusion the letter stated that the Pope was much pleased at his initiative and his proposition.

With the approbation from such high quarters and certain that the Pope "in his fatherly solicitude had deigned to accept his humble suggestion," he launched his pamphlet entitled *Italian Emigration to America.*

In it he stated that he took for granted that emigration from Italy could not nor should be stopped. Hence he felt it necessary to consider it as a human, civic, and patriotic duty, to counsel and warn those unfortunates who were forced to leave Italy against the dangers awaiting them on the long and painful road of exile.

He went on to point out how in Italy nothing had been done in this respect. He exposed the terrible conditions in which the emigrants often found themselves. He concluded by listing a number of practical measures intended to bring help to them, both in a material and moral way. The need was urgent:

1. To protect the prospective emigrants from the shameful speculations of certain emigration agencies, traffickers in human flesh.

2. To create information as well as placement agencies.

3. To furnish aid in case of need, misfortune, or sickness, both during the trip and after landing.

4. To wage an implacable battle against those slave traders in human flesh who do not shrink from using the lowest and the most degrading of methods.

5. To provide religious assistance during the trip, after landing, as well as wherever emigrants establish themselves.

On this last point he spoke at length. In no uncertain terms he brought out the fact that, deprived of any form of religious life, the emigrants of many localities in both North and South America led almost pagan lives which gradually would lead them to absolute religious indifferentism and, as a consequence, to brutish materialism.

Moreover, he brought out the point that where the voice of the Catholic priest was not heard, non-Catholic and Masonic proselytizing would be at work. It was easy to see how in a short time, although a new and prosperous Italy might arise in the two Americas, it would be an Italy suffering from spiritual malnutrition. He pointed out the fact that the Italians tended to establish themselves in colonies, hence the necessity of impressing that religious character upon them on which would depend their future standing.

These short notes are enough to make us understand how the complex situation had been truly studied with "the intellect of love," the intellect of an Italian plus the love of a bishop. His suggestions raised a unanimous chorus of approbation.

The *Osservatore Romano*, as the interpreter of the general sentiment, remarked:

"Bishop Scalabrini has said that the character, Catholic and Italian, to be impressed on the new colonies will be the strongest link with distant Italy. We add that here among us this co-ordinated work between the clergy and the people toward our brethren who are forced to abandon their native land will be a common ground whence to demonstrate more and more that the national and religious interests are one and the same. This opportune drawing closer will not be the last benefit those poor people will send to their native land."

At the same time, to confirm the fact that the problem was not only real but most urgent, and that it was not purely a religious one, the government of Italy endorsed a bill on emigration, presented by Prime Minister Crispi and modified by the Parliamentary Committee, headed by the Honorable Roch De Zerbi.

Bishop Scalabrini considered it his duty to intervene—a duty both as citizen and as churchman. When he examined the two drafts of the proposed bill, he courageously and publicly joined the ranks of those debating and discussing the issues at stake. Moreover, he addressed an "open letter" to the undersecretary of state, the Honorable Paul Carcano, an old schoolmate of his when he was a boy in Como.

Stating as a premise that an open letter to a deputy by a bishop who interested himself in social conditions and proposed bills might be sufficiently important to arouse the current morbid indifference of the public, his letter was clear and to the point. He presented his point of view, praising what to him meant pursuing the right track, and confuting what in his opinion was weak. He made suggestions which he felt had been overlooked and advised the suppression of certain directions which appeared to be inopportune and, in his opinion, even harmful for the emigrants.

The Zerbi Bill, he felt, although far from perfect, was the better one. It sanctioned full liberty to the emigrants, but, at the same time, conceded that agents of emigration should be allowed the right to recruit. Bishop Scalabrini was irrevocably opposed to this last provision and stated his views in eloquent terms.

The Crispi Bill, on the other hand, concerned with the number of abandoned farms, which increased year by year, leaned toward limiting the emigration trend. The bishop advised Crispi to act less as the minister of the interior and more as one gifted with a clear foresight of the future. As a statesman, the minister would not impede but direct the migration trend that it might thus become a source of strength and well-being for the motherland. In conclusion, he warned both sponsors of the bill that a law, no matter how good, is not sufficient. The law must so provide that the general and complex problem of emigration may achieve those high social ends determined by Providence itself. It cannot succeed unless aided by all those wise public and private institutions, religious and civic organizations, which gave so much success to the people who were pioneers in the field.

"Those organizations," he pointed out, "not only encourage the poor emigrants to proceed more confidently along the path they have chosen, since they will feel themselves protected, but make people in foreign countries realize that they are not forgotten, are not 'people of no account,' but part of a great nation that knows its duty and fulfills it, a nation ready to extend the protection of its flag over her distant sons, helping them in their material needs, and lifting their moral character through religion and education."

He explained also to the Honorable De Zerbi that missionaries are best suited to become soldiers, as it were, of Church and country, by applying themselves to the spiritual assistance and the education of their fellow countrymen. And here he added that it had been a grave mistake to deny these men of the Church exemption from military service.

There were those of the Intransigent Party who attacked him with fury. They again raised the cry of scandal on seeing the bishop of Piacenza treat directly with the representatives of the government branded as the "usurper." The Vatican looked upon his step as daring indeed, but was not displeased. On the contrary, the Vatican paper summarized the letter fully. After stating that the illustrious bishop was adding to his many titles of merit acquired by his religious effort, that of dedicating himself wisely and practically to the emigration problem in America, it concluded by stating:

"Is there any need of further praise for the work done by the great prelate and for the words he has written? No, indeed. Rather, we have limited ourselves in quoting the steps he outlines. The ideas of the author demand that they be diffused more than recommended."

The bishop's brother, Angelo, wrote to him from Rome:

"In Parliament everyone is talking about your open letter. As soon as each deputy arrives he congratulates the undersecretary of state, Carcano. I mean all of them, rightists, leftists, and extremists. The Honorable De Zerbi said that he wishes to offer you the praise that is your due in full parliamentary session. The Honorable Roux called your letter a jewel; the Honorable De Vecchi, a sane and vigorous book from the first to the last word. I should never end if I were to quote to you all the words of admiration spoken of you by the members of Parliament. . . ."

Several deputies and senators, in fact, sent him personal congratulatory messages, saying they agreed fully with the ideas he had promulgated.

Even the president, Honorable Biancheri, praised the bishop's words "because they were inspired by noble sentiments of philanthropy and charity in the interest of his country."

At one of the sessions of Parliament he was described as "an illustrious man, one of the most progressive, cultured, and kindly prelates in our land," by the anti-clerical, Honorable Bonfadini.

Everything favored the hopeful supposition that the bishop's point of view and his proposals would be given serious and kind consideration. But the year was 1888. That is, shortly after the hopes for conciliation between the government and the Holy See had fallen on barren ground, due to the Jacobinic Crispi Government. And if it was true that among the Catholics there were many relentless Intransigents, there were no less relentless ones among the anti-clericals. Hence, the *Riforma*, the official government newspaper, exposing its true colors, soon took a position against the bishop by stating that his proposal to provide schools for the emigrants conducted by missionaries, thus exempting the seminarians from military service, could not be accepted. It declared that the reason for this decision was that education offered in the seminaries did not give sufficient guarantee of merit. The *Riforma* maintained that this was proved by mediocre marks received by the seminarians when they took the examinations prescribed by the public system of education. It also did not dissemble its displeasure at the fact that the bishop had given his preference to the bill presented by the committee, rather than to Crispi's proposal which the *Riforma* was bound to support. Evidently the editor did not realize that his claim was absurd because of the fundamental principles which were behind the bill.

On the day following the parliamentary discussion, the letter *Quam Aerumnosa* of December 10, 1888, was sent by the Pope to the American bishops. The letter accentuated the diffidence of the Crispi government toward the bishop of Piacenza, a diffidence probably more simulated than real. In the letter the Pope made the announcement that he directed Bishop Scalabrini to establish a seminary in Piacenza for the training of priests who wished to dedicate themselves entirely to the care of the emigrants.

The *Riforma*, because of this letter, showed its animosity in venomous words. It evinced itself as convinced and fearful that the Pope was attempting, hand in hand with the bishop of Piacenza, to regiment Italian emigration into a Catholic army, directed by and dependent upon priests. It begged the government to open its eyes, insisting that forces organized by the Vatican in foreign lands were not to be trusted. It added that it was hardly fitting for the Italians to present themselves in foreign lands as followers of clericalism!

It might not have been impossible for the Servant of God to placate these outbursts and gain the government's favor so useful to his work. But he was convinced that the new law that the government had in mind would in the end make the condition of the emigrants worse. He would never consent to a lie, whether through cowardice or to gain his own ends. He therefore continued in his disapproval of it. For the moment his ideas had to be held in check. As we shall see, in a short time, however, he was so tenacious, zealous, and irresistible in his efforts, both with his spoken word and his pen, as to make known and focus the attention of all upon the great problem of emigration. Finally his ideas triumphed. He had been the first man in Italy to tackle the problem.

In 1896 a new bill was presented to the Italian Parliament by the Honorable Pantano. In it the question of military service by missionaries was taken up seriously and honestly. But it was not until 1900 that a decisive turn took place, when the Honorable Visconti-Venosta, minister of foreign affairs, introduced a new bill to the Italian Parliament. A parliamentary committee, headed by the Honorable Luzzatti, released a report in which the government was requested to allow greater freedom to the young Italian missionaries who were subject to the draft. The hope was formulated that at least outside of Italy the friction between Church and State would cease, and the Italians in foreign lands be given the comfort of joining into one bond their love of God and country. As for what concerned the recruiting of prospective emigrants from Italy, what Bishop Scalabrini had sustained for twelve long years was recognized as *right!* The bill on the matter, as introduced by the Pelloux Cabinet, became law the following year, when Marquis Starabba di Rudini was the head of the government of Italy. It had been elaborated upon by such outstanding personalities as Pantano, Luzzatti, Lampertico, and Schiapparelli. Bishops Scalabrini and Bonomelli had given their co-operation.

The year before, in Turin, Bishop Bonomelli, urged on by the noble example of his dear friend, and as if to bring his work to a successful completion, had founded the Institute for Assistance to the Italian Emigrants in Europe. Thus did he deserve to have a voice in the matter.

Bishop Scalabrini, invited by the government to give his "precious contribution," sent Father Peter Maldotti to Rome. The latter was in charge of the care of the emigrants at the port of Genoa and had been to Brazil on two different occasions, there to study the conditions under which the immigrants found themselves.

Providence added a third member, one who also was invited to give of his rare experience. He was Commendatore Natale Malnate, inspector of public safety at the port of Genoa. He was a man of great wisdom in the guise of a public officer, and a man of sterling conscience.

Father Maldotti and Inspector Malnate had met each other at the port, where both labored closely for the triumph of goodness and righteousness. They met in Rome, happy in being able to unite their efforts in seeing that the new law which was about to go into effect would respect and honor those high moral and religious principles without which any effort to help the emigrant would resolve itself into a mockery and a betrayal.

CHAPTER 19

Words and Deeds

. . . emigration is a law of nature . . .

WHILE GOVERNMENT OFFICIALS in Rome discussed, harangued, and formulated projects, Bishop Scalabrini, who saw the urgent need of coming to some concrete decision, did something about it. He began by establishing a provisional committee in Piacenza in 1887 which, in turn, elected him president by acclamation.

The committee developed into a society, which came to be known as the St. Raphael Society. Within its folds were brought together on the common ground of Christian charity famous men of opposing political views, the clergy, and the laity. It was modeled on the original St. Raphael Society, a group organized in Germany in 1871 by a wealthy merchant and deputy of Parliament, a missionary, and a nun. Through this society Bishop Scalabrini planned to keep alive in the hearts of the emigrants love of the motherland together with love of their faith. Besides this, he hoped to bring about a better moral, physical, intellectual, economic, and civic well-being for them.

One of the first steps to be taken by the society was to provide financial aid to the emigrants. The society was also to assist missionaries on duty during the crossings, as well as to erect churches and oratories in the various centers of Italian colonies.

Physically, it was to provide medical care and assistance for the emigrants during and after their long voyages. Its intellectual aim was to open schools where the rudiments of the Catholic faith as well as the Italian language were to be taught.

The society's legal assistance would consist of giving advice and help to the emigrants in their dealings with local authorities and with the drawing up of contracts and in fostering good labor relations, in order to prevent speculation by irresponsible agents.

Economically, it was to furnish them with definite information as to the land of their destination, the condition of the soil, climatic conditions, work, etc.

The St. Raphael Society was subdivided into committees. The central committee was to be in Piacenza, while local committees were to be established preferably in places of embarkation, in countries to which the emigrants were bound, in countries that took in greater contingents of emigrants, and in the principal Italian centers.

The bishop was confident of being able to provide economic help for the society through offerings he received.

The first president of the central committee was the Marquis F. B. Volpe Landi, who later dedicated all of his time to this work and who well deserves to be remembered.

The National Aid Society for the Italian Catholic Missionaries, also founded in 1887, with headquarters in Florence, hastened to express its approbation to Bishop Scalabrini for his noble and daring initiative. It saw to it that its members did everything possible to promote his work. Letters of praise and gratitude reached the Apostle to the Emigrants from many cities.

Let us, just for a moment, consider the vast and wise plan for moral and material support conceived by him. Nothing concrete existed at the time to help these poor people who were driven to choose unknown and perilous paths alone, accompanied only by the weight of their sufferings.

The name of Bishop Scalabrini was a guarantee of honest endeavor and success to anyone who knew him.

The first task involved the diffusion of the idea, the establishment of local committees, and finally the collection of necessary funds to turn words into deeds. The idea to be kept alive in Italian hearts was the gravity of the problem and the Christian and patriotic duty of giving aid and comfort. The idea spread, for an idea is like a torch. As long as the torch is held under the bushel, no one sees the light.

Money was sorely needed. It would have been ridiculous to expect it to pour down from heaven. It was much wiser to induce those who need to make friends through the mammon of iniquity in order to enter the kingdom of heaven to dig deep into their pockets and give with generous hearts.

With these thoughts spurring him on and without delay he became the traveling salesman of the emigrants. He went from city to city, speaking on emigration and soliciting funds. He started from Genoa, where most of the emigrants boarded ships that were to take them to the Americas, and where the local committee was already functioning well.

He spoke on January 25, 1891, in the Church of the Magdalen. The archbishop of Genoa was present. Bishop Scalabrini's words in support of his project were so convincing and so touching that the hoped-for result was obtained. The consensus of opinion was favorable, and, what counted most, new members joined the committee and a considerable sum of money was raised.

From Genoa he proceeded to Rome combining with his *ad limina* visit a meeting with a distinguished committee of persons interested in the subject so close to his heart. The conference took place before an exceptionally large audience and its success was stupendous. The Pope received him in private audience and offered his congratulations.

Florence came next, then Turin, and finally Milan, where he concluded his first propaganda journey. The next year he spoke in Lucca, Pisa, Treviso, and Palermo, literally covering Italy from one end to the other. Wherever he went, the results were heart-warming. Public opinion in the cause of the emigrants could not have been awakened with deeper warmth born of conviction, nor with greater competence.

The Servant of God upheld the thought that emigration is a law of nature. "The physical world, as the human world," he read in the stenographic notes of one of his conferences, "is subject to this tremendous force which stirs and mingles the elements of life without destroying them. It transports organisms born in a certain spot and scatters them into space, transforming and perfecting them, thus renewing at every moment the miracle of creation. Seeds migrate on the sweep of the winds, plants are carried along from continent to continent by the currents of sea and river, birds and animals migrate. Even as these does man migrate, now in collective groups and again in isolation, always, however, as an instrument of Divine Providence who presides over human destinies guiding them at times through catastrophic occurrences on to the final destination—that is, the perfection of man on earth and the glory of God in heaven.

"This is what Divine Revelation tells us, this is what history and modern biology teach us. Only by drinking in of this threefold source of truth shall we be enabled to deduce the laws that govern the phenomenon of migration and to establish precepts of practical wisdom that must hold it in line throughout all of its manifold forms.

"These precepts warn us that emigration is a natural and inalienable right and a social safety valve. As such it reestablishes equilibrium between wealth and the productive power of a people. It is a source of well-being for him who leaves and for him who remains behind, relieving a land of overpopulation and putting a higher value on the handiwork of those who remain. It may become a good or an evil thing, individual or national, according to the ways and means by which it is being accomplished. But almost without exception it works for the good of mankind. Thereby new roads are opened to commerce and the diffusion of scientific and industrial findings is made easier when people of diverse minds and capabilities meet and mingle and thus bring about a more perfect civilization. The concept of a homeland beyond material things is made wider in scope, for it makes the world, in a spiritual sense, the homeland of man."

He enumerated the various forms of migration among a civilized people. Emigration, he explained, may be internal, political, economic, agricultural, commercial, and so on. Then drawing the conclusion that "for the present, at least," Italy's problem was an economic one, he asked:

"What, then, are the guarantees the law allows such a type or such types of emigration? How does the state exercise its duty toward caring for the moral and the material welfare of these people? How do we, as leaders, fulfill this duty?"

After putting these questions to himself and then placing them before his listeners, the bishop gave warning of the numberless dangers by which emigration is surrounded. He also pointed out the tremendous evils that follow it. First among these, he stated, was the fault of the emigration agents, comparable to slave traders, who ignobly took advantage of the miserable and the wretched.

The bishop then uncovered the nefarious work done by these termites, and denounced them before the public, comparing them to vampires in old wives' tales who sucked the blood of their victims, as they literally engaged in buying and selling them, and at times even in bringing about the death of souls as well as of bodies.

He explained how duty toward these people and interest in them involved many and important matters, different from one another and yet intimately connected. Whatever concerned the problem of emigration, whether it dealt with religion or nationality, public or private interests, had to be considered as a whole, or damage would result.

Two fundamental ideas were given for the solution of the problem. Emigration had to be protected and well directed. Protection and direction had to resolve themselves into legislative, religious, and philanthropic action, in all of which the government, the clergy, and all good men, no matter to what party they belonged, had to take part.

He examined every item in detail, beginning with the emigration bill, in order that he might explain his reasons for the disapproval of the emigration agents who, unfortunately, had been authorized by the bill itself to swindle the emigrants. He had great hopes that the new bill would remedy the situation. He was critical of the disposition taken regarding military service of the emigrants and of their sons, as well as of the missionaries in general. He spoke at length on the question of the latter, showing how valuable was their work for the benefit of civilization and for the enhancement of the Italian name and culture. Furthermore, he stated, he was asking for no exceptions and no privileges. All he wanted was the possibility of exchanging the few months spent in a barracks for a lifetime apostolate in the interest of God and country.

God and country are the two words that exalted Bishop Scalabrini and about which he wove his plea, inviting all Italians to unite.

He called this "a sublime ideal which takes form and figure, as it were, in the protection of our emigrants and indeed offers the hope of better days for Italy, so that in time God's design for her may be fulfilled."

This was the theme of one of his conferences. Let no one think, however, that he went around Italy monotonously repeating the same words as some orators usually do. The theme was basically the same, but it was discussed and dealt with in its complex meaning, now under one aspect, again under another. There is no doubt that whenever the opportunity presented itself, for illustrating it from its human and spiritual point of view, he was always eloquent beyond words. At times his words assumed a great dramatic quality.

The sincerity with which he voiced his feelings from the very depths of his heart, his living, burning desire for souls, were such that it is not an empty statement to say that he alone succeeded in awakening the government, the people, and the Church, in one word, all Italy to dedicate themselves wholeheartedly to the solution of the problem.

This is the reason why the Freemasons, fearful that aid for the emigrants was to be placed chiefly in the hands of the clergy, began agitating against what they called the Scalabrinian propaganda by the use of methods such as always distinguished them. Opposition and contradictions against the institution also arose from quarters from which it was least expected. There was opposition even against its founder. The bishop ignored the attacks and continued unperturbed. His efforts soon began to be appreciated even outside of Italy.

Proof of this lies in the visit paid the bishop of Piacenza by the Honorable Cahensly, the organizer in Germany of the St. Raphael Society. The two men conferred at great length and Marquis Volpe Landi, president of the Central Italian Committee, joined them in their exchange of views. The aim of the meeting was to establish closer relations between the two societies for the common interest of their countrymen. The German leader also went to Genoa to study the problems concerning the assistance to be given the emigrants and to see how it was applied.

CHAPTER 20

At the Root of the Problem

*. . . initiated the great plan to give
leaders, teachers and companions . . .*

THE St. Raphael Society was a long-range project. But its
work could only be one of support. The committees
did much, but at a distance, and the emigrants needed a
more direct contact, one that was assiduous and continuous.

Bishop Scalabrini had realized this from the start. The
fact that he had been satisfied to begin with the St. Raphael
Society had been because he felt that to gain success only
one step at a time could be taken. The society was the first
step. In his heart even then he envisioned the emigrant accompanied on his way by a man who was free from any other
duty, a man who could dedicate himself utterly to his service. And since the needs of these emigrants were chiefly moral
and religious, and since letters sent from beyond the seas
called for a priest, the conclusion was clear. The need called
for missionaries!

It was not the case of an absolute absence of priests. In
fact, there were a number of priests who offered their services, who even insisted on being sent to exercise their ministry in the Americas. But, lacking the necessary training,
they did not always give good proof of themselves. So in
1890 the Sacred Congregation of the Council prohibited
all Italian bishops from granting any secular priest the authorization to leave for North or South America and asked
American bishops to be on the watch and provide for the
necessary measures to enforce the prohibition. Hence the

141

need for replacing these priests with well-trained and well-disciplined religious became even more urgent. The problem was being studied in Rome.

The German Society of St. Raphael had already shown good results in this respect. Why not try something similar in Italy? All that was needed was a competent, courageous, inspiring leader. And was he not at hand?

We know that the bishop of Piacenza had worked on this project ever since 1887. He had succeeded in arousing the interest of Cardinal Simeoni. Then he had appealed directly to the Pope, who gave thought to it. The bishop's plans were finally approved. An institute for Italian priests in Piacenza resulted. This institute was to be subject to regulations approved by the Sacred Congregation for the Propagation of the Faith. The Italian priests were to be willing to go to America to help the Italian immigrants for a period of at least five years. They were, moreover, to place themselves at the disposal of the local bishops. Bishop Scalabrini was then authorized to procure a building wherein to house the institute. Offerings from friends of the project were to provide for other expenses. The Pope gave orders that a visitor apostolic be sent to America to familiarize himself with the status of the immigrants. He also gave orders for letters to be written to the American bishops asking for needed information and telling them about the plans that were being formulated in Piacenza. Finally he asked that Bishop Scalabrini be notified of his express desire to have the Italian bishops favor the initiative, encourage it, and inspire priests to dedicate themselves to missionary work by entering the institute.

Then he sent a papal brief to the bishops in which he reiterated his ideas. These he had solemnly sanctioned in an encyclical letter to the American bishops in 1889.

The bishop felt strengthened by the august approval of Leo XIII and wrote to his Italian brother-bishops to share the same views. Practically all of them sent assurances of co-operation, congratulation, and financial aid. Hence, he was able to tackle his task serenely and efficiently.

The provisional regulations approved by the Sacred Congregation for the Propagation of the Faith prescribed that the members of the society, after a year of novitiate at the mother house in Piacenza, were to take the usual three religious vows. Then they were to place themselves at the disposal of their superior general. The title of "apostolic missionary" was given to the individual religious who left for America.

As to the compilation of the rules and regulations governing the institute itself, Bishop Scalabrini gave evidence of his outstanding characteristic, the virtue of humility. He took advantage of counsels given him by Father Rondina, S.J. Not content with having received them orally, he asked that they be written down for him. He also requested the appointment of a cardinal as protector, and suggested the name of Augustine Cardinal Bausa, archbishop of Florence, who happened to be an enthusiastic supporter of the emigrants' cause. The Pope was pleased with the request and the name suggested to him and acceded immediately to the bishop's wishes.

As with every work that is great in God's sight the Scalabrini Missionary Congregation began its life in a manner which could hardly have been more humble.

Monsignor Dominic Costa, then pastor of St. Antoninus' in Piacenza, was a priest universally held in high regard for his zeal and his great piety. The bishop called him to his side and begged him to take the position of superior, at least temporarily, until another could be definitely appointed. Monsignor Costa wondered as to the whereabouts of his community. The bishop smiled and presented it to him. It was made up of two priests, Father Joseph Molinari of

Piacenza and Father Dominic Mantese of Vicenza. The monsignor smiled, too. But both smiles were sincere and full of light, for there was not the least shadow of a doubt cast on the fate of the small seed which was being sowed. That seed, favored by God Almighty, was to grow into a mighty tree bearing an abundance of good fruit. Even from that moment the two men were certain that God would never fail them.

When Our Lord called his first disciples to follow Him, He was quick to warn them that the Son of Man, less fortunate than the beast in the forest, had not whereon to lay His head. Likewise the new congregation had no roof under which to gather. Monsignor Costa solved the problem by offering his house.

At noon of November 28, 1887, the Servant of God gathered the ranks of his disciples within the Church of St. Antoninus. There he led them to the tomb of the martyr saint, the holy patron of Piacenza. As superior general he received their first profession. But the doors of the temple were closed, that the people might not wonder at a rite, almost wholly symbolic, the meaning or value of which they could not have fathomed.

Steps were being taken, with the authorization of the Holy See, for the acquisition of a former convent and the church annexed to it—closed at the time—of a small garden along with several rustic buildings. The property had passed into the hands of the diocesan seminary after the suppression of the religious orders, which suppression had taken place after the fall of Rome.

The transaction took too much time for the small seed was beginning to give proof of great hidden vitality. It was decided to transfer the small group to other temporary quarters under the guidance of the superior, Father Bartholomew Rolleri.

Father Rolleri had been a missionary in Central Africa

along with the Servant of God, Bishop Daniel Comboni, another great pioneer of Christ. For many years Father Rolleri had been at the missionary institute in Cairo and had returned to Piacenza only because of his health. He was the very man needed at the moment.

Among the first to join him was Father Francis Zaboglio. As a pastor, this priest had come to know the sad situation among the emigrants on the occasion of a trip he took to America. He had known Bishop Scalabrini for a long time and had an unlimited veneration for him. He believed in the cause and embraced it with enthusiasm. Later he became vicar general of the congregation.

In 1892 the mother house was ready to greet the congregation. Bishop Scalabrini called it Christopher Columbus Institute in homage to the discoverer of the new continent and the first man to plant the Cross on the shores of the New World. He named the congregation Missionaries of St. Charles. The name of St. Charles, he felt, was a standard and a seal. In the saint he saw the model and the protector of his sons.

In 1896 a new building was added to the mother house to be used as a minor seminary for the young men who aspired to the high calling of the missionary life.

As soon as the news of the founding of the new institute had crossed the ocean, the bishop's desk was piled high with letters of praise and with requests for help.

"Now I am breathing easier," wrote Archbishop Michael Augustine Corrigan of New York. "There is hope now for these dear souls who are being lost to us by the thousands. Up to now I could find no way of saving them! Today, I am happy and content. God be praised again and again!"

On July 12, 1888, the first missionary band sailed from Piacenza. It was composed of seven priests and three lay brothers. Two of the priests and one lay brother were as-

signed to New York, two priests with one lay brother to
Santa Felicidade of Curitiba (Paraná, Brazil), and three
priests with the remaining lay brother to the State of Espi-
rito Santo of Brazil.

When the Apostles set out on their way to preach the
"good tidings" to the Gentiles, only a few hundred souls believed in Christ. And yet they felt in their hearts that Christianity meant life. When Peter and Paul entered the city of
Rome, only a few slaves dreamed a vague dream of the Kingdom of God. Only a few people awaited them. All around
stood the crowds ignorant of the truth, the empire with its
armies, its wealth, its rites, and its false gods. And yet neither
Peter nor Paul had a moment's doubt that the salvation of
the world lay in the faith of the Carpenter of Nazareth.
They had no perception of their solitude in this pagan
world, but in their few brethren they felt Christ. And when
they gathered together in brotherhood, they could repeat the
Dominus Vobiscum without any doubt in their souls that
the future belonged to these few and humble neophytes.
Their great faith made them feel the Universal Church present within the small assembly.

Faith such as this was also required of that small group
of heroic men in 1888. They had it. Action along the same
lines was imposed upon many of them if they wanted the
future to be of the sacred ideal that urged them upward.
They were ready to dare all, without fear and without regrets.

They met once again in the basilica of St. Antoninus, the
patron saint of Piacenza. Before the tomb of the martyred
saint they gathered their strength to forge ahead into the
New World. But this time the doors of the basilica were
wide open to the public. And all of Piacenza participated in
the solemn rite, while the whole of Italy, proud of its sons,
joined with them in spirit.

A great Italian, the historian Cesare Cantù, interpreted

the sentiments of the good people of Italy in a letter to the most reverend bishop:

"I beg Your Excellency to add the prayers of an old man, who so much admires the courage and the sense of abnegation of the missionaries for the Italian emigrants, to the blessings you are calling down upon them on this day of their departure. I beg it of you who have initiated and promoted the great work which is giving leaders, teachers, and companions to those Italians who have been forced to leave their native land in search of bread. The world may have the levity of not recognizing them, the ingratitude to forget them, but they will proceed onward in their mission, the Cross their banner; their battle cry: 'Christ today, tomorrow, and forever.' "

And thus it was.

CHAPTER 21

Struggles and Victories

. . . the St. Raphael Society priests, missionaries, men and women of the world, working together toward a worthy cause . . .

AMONG the local committees of the St. Raphael Society the one in Genoa was the most efficient. This was due not only to the general atmosphere of the place but to the men and women who dedicated themselves with so praise-worthy a spirit of selflessness to the work which had to be done. Hence, it deserves our particular praise, since its intense and multiform action helps us better to understand what Bishop Scalabrini's intentions were in promoting the missionaries' efforts and in placing them wherever they would be most needed.

The Genoa committee of the society fulfilled two important functions. One was legal and social, aiding the local emigration boards in the protection and assistance of the emigrants. The other dedicated itself to charitable purposes, in union with the Italica Gens, a benevolent association inspired by Professor Ernest Schiapparelli, and also with the Genoese Women's Group, which furnished the needy emigrants with clothing. These two groups aided about 100,000 emigrants a year.

Bishop Scalabrini understood almost from the beginning that only one of his missionaries could give life and energy and soul to an enterprise of so great importance, since he was bound to it by the duties of his sacred ministry. Thus

148

in 1891 he sent Father Zaboglio to Genoa. We have mentioned this great priest before. In 1894 he sent Father Maldotti, a born apostle, to succeed him.

Bishop Scalabrini opposed the recognition of the agents and assistant agents of emigration with all his powers. It would have been necessary to work at the port of Genoa to understand his reasons for this attitude.

We are not going to say that all of these agents were profiteers, but the majority were misplaced men of all types who somehow had succeeded in getting a license by shrewd and surreptitious methods. They wandered about the countrysides and practically blackmailed the miserable and the hungry. With exaggerated promises they persuaded them to leave the country, their only aim being to exploit them and make money for themselves and their bosses. Exploitation and speculation were exercised in a thousand ways.

They speculated on the price of transportation which often was doubled and redoubled. They obtained railroad fare reductions by arranging for special trains, charging the regular fare, and dividing the difference in price with the organizers of their traffic in human flesh. They arranged for overnight reservations, receiving a percentage from owners of inns and boarding houses for each victim of the trap. Finally they made money on deposits paid for "unforeseen expenses." Of course, under one pretext or another, the deposits were never returned.

Bled white by these heartless and insatiable scoundrels, some of the emigrants exhausted their small fortunes, put together with so many sacrifices. Perhaps household objects, furniture, or other possessions had been sold. Worse, the money might have been borrowed from unscrupulous moneylenders. It happened that at times nothing would be left; their baggage would then be "attached" and often they became public charges after nights spent in the open.

In the inns they were jammed promiscuously in filthy

rooms, without light or air. The food served them was insufficient and of the worst quality. Nothing was of the highest, except the price that had to be paid without question—and with thanks.

The moneylenders also took advantage of ignorance. And there were even those who exploited the poverty and the desperation of these people to gain unmentionable goals.

A web was spun which was truly infernal. Today it seems impossible to us that such things could have happened and could have been done so brazenly. We cannot understand how responsible authorities could be so careless about such crimes being perpetrated, and yet these things happened. Many, if not all, saw what was going on. But none stopped to think of finding a remedy for the scandal.

Alone, against them all in Genoa, Father Maldotti came to the rescue. Shortly afterward he was assisted by Father Glesaz and by the providential help of the police commissioner, Malnate.

Young, strong, alert, and a good speaker, Father Maldotti went all out against these exploiters. He applied the French saying to the case: "In a war, use war's weapons." He fought them everywhere and in every possible manner. At railroad stations he stood on guard, meeting every incoming train. Acting as a policeman, he denounced to the commissioner of police all those guilty of abuse or any swindling he was able to discover. Each day, it can be said, he had some of the perpetrators fined and sued. He fought the battle so implacably that in a short time he began to receive anonymous letters threatening harm and even death to him and his accomplices. However, seeing that their threats had no effect on him, they went to the prefect of the province and accused those priests as disturbers of the peace, men who had come to interfere with the progress of commerce and of small merchants. An assembly of tradesmen and

shopkeepers, presided over by a number of well-known Freemasons, proceeded to hurl public denunciations against them
to the authorities!

How was this daring move to be met? Advised by the
police commissioner, the two missionaries decided to appeal
to the newspapers! They offered to expose important information on the situation. The papers of the time, just as
they are today, were only too anxious to make headlines with
some sensational bit of news. They accepted the offer. The
paper *Caffaro*, the first to give the news, immediately announced the publication of a series of articles in eyecatching
advertisements—"Mysterious Happenings at the Port and
Scandalous Exploitation of the Emigrant." Other papers
quickly followed suit. With the speed of lightning the newspaper campaign spread in a series of stirring articles to which
was added the weight of documentary proof.

Then began a deluge of libel suits for defamation of
character, but that is as far as it went. In the meantime, the
authorities, indirectly but nonetheless openly, called upon
to settle matters and forced to open their eyes, began to take
the situation seriously. Investigations were made and the
offenders punished without any show of mercy. The prefect
of Genoa, awakened too late from his lethargy, was transferred. And the transfer had all the appearance of a well-
deserved punishment. Regulations were adopted which had
been begged for uselessly for a long period of time and, as
a result, agents were prohibited from sending for the emigrants until the day preceding their departure free of charge.
The press, which often serves causes far from good, this
time gave splendid service to a splendid cause. And it
crowned that service with astounding success.

No sooner had one obstacle been surpassed, however,
than another rose to take its place. As soon as the emigrants
arrived in Genoa, they were immediately put on board ship

without having been submitted to a medical examination. This meant serious danger during the crossing. Infectious diseases had ample time to develop. Once on the high seas they manifested themselves with due consequences. One can easily imagine what occurred.

Up until 1891 Bishop Scalabrini had insisted that a lodginghouse be built at all ports of embarkation. There the emigrants could be housed, examined, cleansed from infection, fed, and assisted in every possible manner. The Marquis Del Carretto, faithful interpreter of the bishop's aims, and a fast worker, had already begun the building of one of these lodginghouses in Genoa. Unfortunately, he died suddenly, and after his death the project was dropped.

Bishop Scalabrini appealed to the government, and succeeded in having the law of 1901 enforce the building of an emigrants' shelter at every port of embarkation. Notwithstanding the fact that the emigrant committee, instituted on the heels of the law, had at its disposal the sum of 10,000,-000 lire, gathered from the emigration tax, nothing was done to fulfill the order.

It is easy to see that no matter how much is said and done, the world and its people do not change much through the years.

Meanwhile the port of Genoa mission had been strengthened and accepted. The missionary was feared by the profiteers and appealed to by the needy. Both Father Maldotti and Father Glesaz were at the station upon the arrival of any trainload of emigrants and took them in charge. They lined them up, closed ranks, and led them through the streets to the port station, closely watched and guarded. There were times when they had to struggle against the blackguards who tried hard to lead some of the travelers astray. It was a common sight to see the two missionaries bearing children in their arms or helping old people or invalids along the way.

On the following morning they would return to the piers. There were times when a child born during the night had to be baptized, or one who had passed away blessed and prepared for burial.

It happened also, and not too rarely, that some individuals could not leave on a scheduled ship. Left to their own devices, they wandered away. The battle against the agents and the innkeepers began once more. Hungry and desperate, these unfortunates would appeal for aid and find it at the lodginghouse of the missionaries.

Another obstacle! Non-Catholic groups filtered into Italy and began their attempts to proselytize the Italian emigrants. They promised and they suggested. One of their arguments was that since they were seeking work in America, a Protestant country, it might be easier for them to find such work there if they were to join one of the many sects in that country.

Father Maldotti went to work against this new problem. Again he fought, and again he won. What he had to accomplish was painstaking work. Each day brought a new situation which had to be battled against. And hard. Soon their resources dwindled.

One day Father Maldotti was at a loss as to how to fulfill the promises he had made. He and his companion were unable to pay for their daily needs. His faith in the Blessed Mother saved the day. On his knees he spoke to her as a son to his mother:

"Most Holy Mother, if you want us to keep on assisting these poor souls who are the beloved of your Divine Son, provide for them and for us also. What shall we do otherwise?"

And the Blessed Mother did provide. Help came in the form of a large offering such as to permit the two missionaries to pay all their bills and continue their work of mercy. Father Glesaz was then sent to America and Father Maldotti was left alone. Little by little not only did he become the unchallenged spiritual head of the emigrants, but also one who was looked up to in reverence by the ship captains and by the sailors who manned the boats. Even the government recognized the wonder of the work he was accomplishing by honoring him with the cross of the Knights of the Crown of Italy.

A further urgent necessity was that of providing religious assistance to the emigrants during the crossings, which at times took as long as a month.

It was a month of forced inactivity in the narrow quarters of the third-class accommodations. Men, women, and children lived close together, and it is not hard to understand what such promiscuity brought about. Modesty, education, morality were certainly not helped in any way. Only the presence of a priest, not that of mere guards, could help the sad situation—a priest, who with his word, his presence, and his example could hold in check what might easily develop into shameful and dangerous action.

Infectious diseases sometimes broke out. Once during a crossing thirty-nine persons had died. The presence of a priest was certainly needed at such a time.

Bishop Scalabrini tried to provide for this need also within the means he had at hand. The number of his missionaries at the time were few. All of them had to be assigned to important work. The matter called for action on his part. He sent out an urgent appeal to all priests to consecrate some of their time to a trip to America and back and thus aid in the work. They were to be temporary missionaries of the congregation he had founded. He also wrote to the shipping lines and asked them for free passage for these priests sailing on ships carrying emigrants aboard. He obtained his request and succeeded in giving his beloved charges a guardian angel, as it were, in the person of a priest.

So many people helped to alleviate the hardships of the emigrants that soon after both the Italian and the American press wrote in glowing terms of this great work, naming it "true and practical patriotism."

The *Comune,* a Piacenza newspaper, hardly one that could be suspected of clericalism, wrote on the departure of one of the Piacenza priests in this sound vein:

"Face to face with this evil of emigration, an evil which it is impossible for us to prevent, the national sense of righteousness suggests and imposes the duty of doing at least what we morally are able to do in order to lessen its sad consequences.

"Governments have tried it. But their action, based only on the high-sounding phraseology of a bureaucracy happily in power, has remained sterile and fruitless.

"The Church set to work. More farseeing, practical, and efficient, it added deeds to mere words. . . .

"It is useless to deny it. The bishop of Piacenza has written a luminous page in the annals of emigration. He is the man who has added to his words, the most efficient means to give them value . . . practical, steadfast, constant action."

This is judgment of particular value. For when the enemies of the Church and clergy, usually so bitter, are led to give favorable recognition to work done by a bishop, it must be taken as a sign that this work is manifesting itself clearly and outstandingly under the pitiless light of day!

CHAPTER 22

People the Same the World Over

. . . the beginnings . . .
new life . . . new hopes . . .

THE CARE of the immigrants during the ocean crossings from Italy to the Americas was certainly a holy cause, though it was not of primary importance in the general picture of the initiatives already working in their favor.

Bishop Scalabrini, if he had lived longer, would no doubt have made wide provisions for it. At the time of its inception, however, he could not easily dispose of his missionaries, few as they were, by separating them from their real field of endeavor in North and South America. It is true that in Italy the situation was as yet not too good, but in America, as far as the immigrants were concerned, things were not much better. If in Italy these unfortunates were exploited and swindled, the same devilish net was being woven here by unscrupulous men. It extended itself even to the children. These were given low jobs in factories and stores, with long hours and miserable pay. Women also were caught by golden promises of honest work and then discouraged and snared into lives of sin.

The tentacles of this exploitation began at the landing port. Bishop Scalabrini thus became interested in stymying the schemes of these traders in human beings through the establishment of the St. Raphael Society which would take these poor people under its protection as soon as they arrived, preventing them from falling victims of their own inexperience. But it must not be forgotten that the immigrants as soon as they left the ship had to pass a physical examination by the inspectors charged with the application of the federal laws governing immigration. As a result of this examination some of the immigrants were held from entering their new land until relatives or friends came to claim them, or until they received adequate means to continue their journey. If a certain period of time passed and no help came, they would be sent back to the country of origin, or referred to a special office of information or, if ill, sent to a hospital set aside for them. It was impossible not to take an interest in these unfortunates until a solution be found or the means provided for their return.

Since at that time there was no direct line from Italy to the United States except to New York, New York had to take a hand.

Bishop Scalabrini sent Father Peter Bandini to that city. As soon as the latter learned of the conditions and the dangers which awaited these people, in agreement with Archbishop Corrigan of New York, he instituted there the St. Raphael Society and set to work. Although charged with the spiritual care of the immigrants in that part of New York that later became the parish of Our Lady of Pompei, Manhattan, Father Bandini did not stop there. Every ship arriving from Italy saw him at the piers. Whatever was necessary for the immigrants he did with a courage and a selflessness that were only equaled by his ability. So much so that in a short space of time he achieved comforting results.

As a representative of the St. Raphael Society he was able to take his place in the immigration office at the port for the purpose of coming to the aid of the incoming crowds from Europe. He overcame difficulties, far from few and far from small, and also succeeded in opening a labor office, for the exclusive use of the Italian immigrant. It functioned much in the same way as the present office of the same kind. To get an idea of its importance and of its great active power, in one year it took care of as many as 20,000 workers.

Then in 1896 Father Bandini had to leave for Texas. The society, deprived of his ability to do almost anything, declined. So badly, in fact, that it was considered a better move to let it die out, rather than to cure it. Bishop Scalabrini, however, realizing the disastrous consequences of such a move, did not allow this to take place. He appealed to the father provincial of North America, Father Gambera, and begged him to do what he could. Father Gambera did not refuse. Not only did he give new life to the society but he succeeded in founding an immigrant house for those who were held at the port of landing as well as a shelter for mothers and young women who were unemployed and without means of support.

In 1908 Father Gambera had to leave this important field of endeavor, as he was called away to be pastor of the large parish of St. Maria Addolorata in Chicago. But the association was now on a solid basis and there was nothing more to fear.

Ever since 1901 the need for providing for our Italian immigrants had also been felt in Boston, Massachusetts, where they were flocking in ever-increasing numbers. But when a shipping line established direct service from Italy to that city it was realized that steps must be taken quickly to provide for them. There also a St. Raphael Society was established, under the honorary presidency of the archbishop of Boston and directed by Father Biasotti, pastor of the Church of the Sacred Heart. Considerable difficulties arose, caused by preconceived ideas as well as diffidence on the part of the civil authorities. And then again—success in full! The clear, peaceful success of good works, which must always strive and battle, but which always end in triumph, to everyone's satisfaction, even that of their former opponents.

In fact, even the authorities were happy, and congratulated themselves for what they had done for the Italian immigrants, and in a special way for foundlings and for abandoned children.

These were laudably provided for by a special committee. Splendid work was also done for delinquents in restoring them to a better and more moral way of life.

Sad to say, in 1908 the missionaries of Bishop Scalabrini, overburdened by the great work of caring for almost 25,000 members of their parish, and poorly helped by the Italian Government, had to forego the management of this benevolent work. They decided to place the work of the organization in the capable hands of Miss Eleanor Colleton, the president of the committee, but at the same time they gave greater expansion to the people's secretariat. This was another form of labor assistance which proves how daring and modern these pioneers really were. Through it they also continued the care of children and young people, and although indirectly they collaborated with the government of Italy in helping as much as they could. And this was the government that, obsessed with the idea of the danger of clericalism, had once worked against them! Which goes to prove once again how charity, generous and kind, even when ill-treated and misused, can and does win over the most ignorant and stubborn sectarianism.

CHAPTER 23

Other Shores, Other Customs

. . . welcomed as a citizen
. . . and as a brother . . .

IN ORDER to grasp the full scope of the plan formulated by Bishop Scalabrini in the interest of the Italian emigrant it may be well for us to cast a rapid glance at the places where his help and advice were sorely needed—help and advice which meant not only assistance of a religious nature, but of a social and civic one as well. Hence the strategy to be employed in achieving any degree of success had to adhere strictly to a sense of reality to conditions and to a wide view.

The conditions in which the Italian immigrants found themselves in that vast world called the Americas were such at the end of the last century that they cried out for a solution to the problem of how to help them.

The countries of North America differ from those of South America especially from the religious point of view. Let us, for the time being, consider North America and, more specifically, the United States of America.

Bella V. Dodd, the famed convert from communism, in her autobiography (*School of Darkness*, P. J. Kenedy & Sons) tells us that she was born in Italy in 1904, baptized Maria Assunta Isabella Visono, and at the age of six came to America with her family from a farm near Potenza.

In the settlement and drifting away from the church of her family emerges a pattern of the lot of most of the Italian families who migrated to the United States.

"We had neighbors all about us—Scotch, Irish, and German families. There were two Catholic churches not far from us. . . . We did not seem to belong to either church and Father and Mother soon ceased to receive the Sacraments and then stopped going to church. But Mother still sang songs of the saints and told us religious stories from the storehouse of her memories.

"Though we still considered ours a Catholic family, we were no longer practicing Catholics. Mother urged us children to go to church but we soon followed our parents' example. I think my mother was self-conscious about her poor English and lack of fine clothes. Though the crucifix was still over our beds and Mother burned vigil lights before the statue of Our Lady, we children got the idea that such things were of the Italian past and we wanted to be Americans. Willingly, and yet not knowing what we did, we cut ourselves off from the culture of our own people and set out to find something new."

The men, women, and children who migrated here from their small, peaceful villages, countryside, or mountaintop, were accustomed to measuring their daily routine by the sound of their church bell. Traffic for them was more or less represented from field or market place. All at once they were flung into the hustle and bustle of a huge metropolis, which even in those years was intense and awesome with noise and confusion. The result was a feeling of utter loss—the feeling of being in a crowd and yet alone, of being helpless among people whose language they did not understand and who could not comprehend them or their ways, whose customs were so different and so strange. They became disoriented, discouraged, frightened, sometimes even rebellious.

Where was the church? They had been told that in America there was a Protestant church and that of churches as they knew them there were none. And if the churches were there, where and how were they to be found amid all that racket? Thus in spite of the fact that a Catholic church might have been a stone's throw away, these people somehow made themselves believe that it was a far-distant nowhere. And so they came to the conclusion that the Church had been left behind with all the dear memories of old, far, far behind, beyond that "big puddle" which they had crossed. Little by little they stopped seeking and resigned themselves to the void, and then, unfortunately, they forgot it altogether.

Some of them were held back because they had been told that in America you had to pay in order to go to Mass; some were deterred by ridicule as to the way they dressed or even prayed. Simple, ignorant country people that they were, they believed what they heard and could not make head nor tail out of it. If we think of these things, it will not be too difficult for us to be charitable and try to understand how hard it must have been for these poor, abandoned souls to adjust themselves to life as it was led in the United States. Here, no religion is the official one. Everyone is permitted freedom of cult but is also expected to provide funds for the exigencies of circumstances, such as supplying funds for the building of places of worship and the maintenance of priests and missionaries.

Today things have changed. Education has spread, people are more emancipated and independent, even in smaller communities. Gone is the fear of losing one's way. Few suffer from overtimidity. In those days, however, that is how matters stood. Lonely and lost in the *mare magnum*, the boundless empty sea of a strange city, where everything, even the most insignificant, was so much bigger than they, those immigrants sorely needed someone who could look after them, comfort them.

This is what the Scalabrinian Missionaries understood. And that is why they set out to do what seemed impossible. Not only did they approach the immigrants, but they mingled with them and lived their meager existence. They shared their needs and their hardships, eating as sparingly as they, and dwelling in as humble abodes, all in accordance with the precept of evangelical poverty, which they had professed.

The profound union between the missionary and the immigrants permitted the former to discover the secret for their regeneration and salvation, close as he was to their lives, to their very souls. The establishment of national parishes was a great contribution to the moral, spiritual, and social adjustment of Italians in the United States.

The Scalabrinians, sent by their founder from Italy, were a link between the American bishops and the Catholic Italian immigrants. First and foremost they organized as best they could large groups in the principal cities. They sought for the best way to keep these people loyal to their religion and to eliminate certain existing frictions among them. Experience and time prove the success of their efforts. They coaxed the immigrants to forget their differences, pull together, and raise a church of their own. The common efforts in building their own church turned out to be a spiritual and social bond. The immigrants of the Italian communities often found themselves united in their needs and in their different activities. The petty antagonism which might have existed, say, between Sicilians or Neapolitans, or between northern or southern Italians became gradually a thing of the past.

A parish church awakened sympathy and co-operation among the people. Common sacrifices were to be met and shared and overcome by all for the fulfillment of a common task. The erection of their own church bound them to become acquainted with one another, engendered exchanges of opinions, made them brothers. A feeling of pride and achievement rendered them worthier sons and daughters of the country of their origin as well as of the country of their adoption.

Side by side with other nationalities, the Italians began to feel themselves more at home in the new environment. The sense of pride in their national origin and in their religious beliefs became a powerful factor in their moral and social development.

This new solidarity also brought about generous response whenever aid was needed, whether in Italy or in the United States, no matter when or how misfortune raised its ugly head. With their missionaries as their leaders, the Italians who had been fortunate enough to better their condition answered generously any appeal for help for their less fortunate brethren. The concept that the Italians were a nation of beggars and filthy wretches, a concept which unfortunately they had acquired when they had first reached the New World, began to wane.

The Scalabrinians worked also in the field of education. The parochial schools that rose one by one in the shadow of the Church safeguarded the religious flame, cornerstone of a healthy, moral education, and also aided in the development of the new citizen.

The national parishes and their schools proved wrong the opinion of some in the matter of assimilation. Such parishes and schools, far from hampering, created and fostered the ideal atmosphere for the process of assimilation. They educated the immigrants and their children to adjust themselves to life in the United States and to become citizens of whom it could be proud.

Every man, although he is an integral part of the whole human race, is born and grows up in a definite environment, that is a nation, a region, a city, or a village. And of this environment that is his own he is bound to magnify customs and characteristics. In fact, he will usually show a certain jealous pride in them. He who is born and has lived most of his life in a given spot—and the truth of this is well known —is apt to undervalue the customs and habits of other regions and other people. Often he is led to criticize them and even go so far as to ridicule them. Sad, yes, but too true. Criticism and ridicule are indulged in not because they are deserved, but simply because the critic knows his own customs intimately, while of the others he knows nothing except the outside covering.

This is all the more deleterious and deplorable when the individuals are from the same country of origin. They possess the same fundamental qualities, they nurture the same principles of religion and of family life, yet they continue to consider themselves as different from those who have sprung from other regional parts of the same country. It is an aftermath of a silly, ingrained localism. Too often the common man is led to attach an exaggerated sense of importance to those external facts which are seen and heard and fire his imagination.

Many people measure and judge the success of a religious celebration by the decorations, the lights, and the music, rather than by the number of the faithful who approach the communion rail. Many are prouder of their city because the local baseball team wins the pennant than because of its achievements through patience and devotion to an ideal by intellectual geniuses or by saintly men. Of this we cannot be duly proud, but we can easily understand it. It is a common failing. Since childhood we have been accustomed to find enthusiastic approval for what takes place in our surroundings rather than within our souls.

Hence we may say that to educate a man who has little or no education, one who, moreover, is worn out and dulled by heavy, arduous, and monotonous work, and to awaken within him love and enthusiasm for the essential things of the spirit, is a task involving the work of much more than a single day. It certainly cannot be achieved by a simple imposition of facts. The psychological personality is formed slowly and gradually. He who sets out to rebuild it, to remold it, must proceed likewise. Hastening matters along, he would arouse the suspicion that he was ready almost to do violence to the person in order to achieve his result. This would create a sense of diffidence and a type of reaction attaining exactly the opposite effect.

We may wish to see the immigrant with his mentality, his moral and spiritual outlook become quickly an integral part of the new homeland. However, the general psychological principles established above explode the theory of a hasty and, at the same time, healthy assimilation. The first aim should be to bring about in the immigrant a smooth and harmonious understanding between the essential values innate in him and those he meets in his new environment. He must be slowly, kindly, and yet firmly persuaded to slide over secondary differences which cannot and should not form an element of discord.

In order to arrive at this ideal state, the immigrant need not be asked to renounce all of his old ideas. At the same time society should meet him halfway. Thus the new and old will merge without any loss of respect in a spirit of mutual understanding and good will toward one another. The immigrant will become convinced that in the new community of which he is now a member he is not a stranger tolerated, but a welcomed citizen and brother. He feels that he is a person toward whom no one will act in a spirit of superiority or contempt, or of whom exaggerated and arbitrary renunciations are demanded.

All this must be achieved gradually. This point should be stressed. No one is easily disposed toward denying his own ego. Anyone attempting to force this will not succeed. Besides, this would bring about the failure of the natural and historical function of migration, which lies in promoting civilization by blending elements of different cultures.

There are those who are of the opinion that assimilation would be easier if the immigrant were to be completely immersed and, as it were, swallowed up in the new environment wherein he has chosen to live. Their opinion also is a superficial and erroneous one. Ignorant of the language, of laws, and of customs, unable to understand or to be understood, the immigrant would soon find himself alone and isolated, a hermit in a crowd. He would helplessly battle against unscrupulous speculators, in any clime and under any sky, lying in wait to take ignoble advantage of the weak, the unwary, the credulous, and the unprotected. He would end up being suspicious not only of men, but of institutions as well. He would hold the society he lives in, not only alien to him but his actual enemy if he felt himself looked down upon as inferior because of his lack of knowledge, and of worldly goods, if suspicion seeped in him that he is unjustly accused and despised because he is not a native.

These elementary reflections point out that in order to ease for any immigrant the assimilation longed for the gap must be bridged between the newcomer and the community which has opened its doors to him.

The Scalabrinian missionaries, under the leadership of their founder, found the solution. They spanned the gap by gathering the immigrants around parishes rooted in the traditions of their national origin. Churches, schools, and societies grew and flourished, where a friendly atmosphere was created naturally, where the immigrants felt at home. There they heard their native language spoken, while at the same time they learned a new one. Their questions were answered in a way they could understand. Through the medium of their own tongue they could acquaint themselves with the new laws, customs, and ideas. With accurate knowledge, correctly learned, they not only became accustomed to the new surroundings, but soon they grew to admire and then to love them. There they met the priests they had known of old, they approached them without fear or timidity. They knew that their ways were not strange and foreign to those priests, nor were some of their weaknesses. They knew that some of their religious manifestations, their traditional way of showing fervor, would not be ridiculed by the same priests even if at times they had to be restrained because of exaggerations or bad taste. They felt that the disapproval of their priests was an understanding, and a sympathetic one. The national parish societies were made up principally of men and women with similar background, and the immigrants consequently did not suffer from that feeling of inferiority which humiliates and discourages. Their opinions could be aired and freely discussed, because they were an integral part in the life of the parish. They gladly welcomed the idea of having their children attend the parish school, where, along with the old, they were able to learn the new life stretching out before them.

Through their assimilation into the life of the national parishes the immigrants acquired a new outlook on the land to which they had come, pressed by the need of earning a less meager living. That land was no longer foreign soil to them, it had become a well-loved second fatherland.

The dreams came true of the Scalabrinian Fathers who were, since the beginning, steadfast custodians of moral and spiritual values in the communities of the Italian immigrants to whom they had dedicated their service.

Missions, churches, schools, parishes among the immigrants did not spread and rise by magic. They claimed a heavy toll: oppositions, tears, sweat, and arduous work. The story of the missionaries of the Italian immigrants, like the story of all those colonizing for Christ, is sown with thorns, with courage, with storm and flood and fire, even with death.

CHAPTER 24

Faith, Courage, and Achievement

. . . by leaps and bounds . . .

THE SCRIPTURAL DICTUM "Flood waters could not quench the fires of charity" comes to mind at the beginning of this chapter. Many times over, as we shall see, it was fire that seemed bent on destroying the work of the Scalabrinians in the United States. It is only natural to wonder at the meaning of this tragic characteristic, a sort of flaming emblem as it were. The answer? We shall not permit ourselves to play with phantasy. Poetry is one thing, history another. And this is history, the history of a great leader inspiring an unshakable band of men with a faith so unquenchable that it achieved success even in the face of opposition by the very elements themselves.

The Scalabrinians arrived in New York City in 1888, and the Italians of that city rejoiced at their coming. They began by renting an empty warehouse and transforming it into a chapel. In that modest abode they sowed their first seed. The Italians of the neighborhood flocked around them. Church attendance increased steadily and never showed a downward trend, even in days of crisis.

This small church continued to function in the interest of the Italian immigrants for a whole year. In the meantime, Bishop Scalabrini saw his family in Piacenza growing in number and making it possible for him to send more of its members across the ocean to aid in the growing work.

In New York City a plan was launched to find a larger and a more fitting place of worship. Twenty years before a

Protestant congregation had built a church on Roosevelt Street. As the years passed, the neighborhood around the church was taken over by the Italians and the others moved away. The property belonging to the church was bought by an Italian who in turn sold it to the Scalabrinians. A down payment of $10,000 was accepted and a long-term mortgage acquired. This was the beginning of the church of St. Joachim. During that first year $20,000 was collected and although a similar amount could not be expected every year, hopes ran high. However, the poor financial ability of the first administrative head brought about a serious crisis. Then, to make matters worse, in November of 1893 a fire broke out in the basement of the church which caused damage to the amount of $12,000 to the church itself.

The colony did not lose courage. Face to face with these misfortunes, it continued to struggle and work through the love it felt for its parish. In a few years the Church of St. Joachim was on a solid financial basis, and in 1913 it celebrated its twenty-fifth anniversary. The parish could boast of a splendid church, a comfortable rectory, a small auditorium for theatricals, and a hall where it gathered the children of the neighborhood for fun and relaxation.

In 1908 Father Vincent Jannuzzi, the new pastor of St. Joachim, on the advice of Mother Cabrini, of whom we shall hear again later, opened a chapel on Catharine Street which was to take care of the Italians living on the East Side. In 1925 this humble chapel gave way to a half-million-dollar project which comprised a church, its rectory, a school, a convent, and an auditorium. The church, located at the corner of Catharine and Monroe streets, was erected as a distinct parish under the tutelage of St. Joseph.

Other churches and chapels soon followed. Among them was the soon flourishing parish of Our Lady of Pompei, the first church in the United States bearing that name. It was located on Bleecker Street. Here, as had been the case on

Roosevelt Street, the building which became a Catholic church had been a Protestant place of worship. The tiny church increased its membership rapidly. In 1913, when not yet twenty-five years old, it could boast of 25,000 parishioners. A fire caused serious damage in 1898 and cost the life of one man and dangerously impaired the health of its great pastor, Father Zaboglio, vicar general of Bishop Scalabrini. Disregarding the precarious condition of his health, Father Zaboglio worked on for more than ten years. He saw the parish of Our Lady of Pompei grow steadily in size and importance. The surrounding neighborhood which for years had become known as a "den of thieves and a den of iniquity" began to change. The change was slow but it was sure. In time it lost what may be designated as its dubious reputation. Father Zaboglio and his energetic assistants saw their efforts blessed by God. But the hardships of those long years finally took their toll of the valiant soldier of Christ, and Father Zaboglio was forced to return to Italy, where he died a holy death in 1911.

In 1926, because of the construction of the New York subway, the old church had to be torn down. The new pastor, the very popular Antonio Demo, in less than four years erected a new and magnificent temple with its rectory, school, convent, auditorium, and gymnasium, at the corner of Carmine and Bleecker streets. The city of New York, in grateful acknowledgment of Father Demo's foresightedness, courage, and spirit of dedication, honored his memory by calling the square facing the church, Demo Square.

From New York City the Scalabrinians reached out into New York State. In Buffalo an Italian colony had existed since 1870. Most of these immigrants had come from Piacenza and Genoa. In later years others came there from southern Italy, and in 1890 the number of Italians living there was 30,000. Their economic status was good, and many had become successful. They owned their own homes and were able to give their children a good education. Their social position was a fair and comfortable one.

It was natural that they should desire to have a church of their own and an Italian priest. Assisted by Father Kofler, a Hungarian priest who knew the Italian language and who had been their standby through the years, they tried to organize a mission parish, but because of their small number this effort had negative results. Again they tried, and again they were unsuccessful. In 1888 Bishop Ryan gave them a chapel in the cathedral and appointed Father James Quigley to assist them. Father Quigley had studied in Rome and knew their language.

The Italians worked diligently at collecting funds for the building of a church. Property was bought and paid for. At this time the provincial of the Scalabrinian missionaries in New York was invited to give a mission in preparation for inaugurating the new parish. He was so impressed by his visit there that he wrote to Bishop Scalabrini about it. The latter immediately sent two of his missionaries there. They went to work with their usual alacrity.

Six months later, in 1891, the building was finished. The lower floor housed the missionaries and the parochial school. The upper floor was given over to the church, dedicated to St. Anthony of Padua.

Offerings continued to pour in, and splendid results thus crowned the efforts that had been put into the great project. By 1912 the parish of St. Anthony had spread, more buildings had risen, and the whole community had prospered.

The story of what happened in Buffalo can be repeated about Syracuse, and also Utica. Divine Providence was certainly standing by its missionaries.

In New England as well as in New York the Scalabrinians were most active. Churches were opened in Boston,

Everett, Framingham, and Somerville, after many years of struggles against opposition and misunderstanding. Later other churches rose throughout the state of Massachusetts.

In New Haven, Connecticut, the Church of St. Michael the Archangel opened its doors in 1889 and was offered to Bishop Scalabrini. Again, as in so many other instances, two missionaries came from Piacenza. The same struggles, the same sacrifices, and the same success followed. In 1897 the first church built became too small and a larger one took its place. Sad to relate, a fire of dubious origin burned it to the ground. The day before this happened, a great religious celebration had taken place there. The archbishop of Hartford had honored it with his presence. The mayor and the civic authorities also were present. It had been a day of great rejoicing. On the following day nothing but blackened, smoking ruins marked the spot.

The church and other buildings had been destroyed, but not the spirit of the missionaries and the people. One year later a new edifice stood ready and waiting. The debt incurred was gradually wiped out. In 1905 a children's shelter was opened together with a school and a third building where young girls were taught sewing and embroidery. In 1923 a new and magnificent building was dedicated to gather together all these projects. Therein was also to be found an association of young men working and striving toward better citizenship in an atmosphere of brotherly understanding. They had their own auditorium, with a stage for theatricals, conferences, etc. Later an orphans' home was added under the supervision of the Zelatrice Sisters of the Sacred Heart.

In order to take care of the Italians living at a distance from St. Michael's, the Scalabrinians began the construction of St. Anthony's Church on Gold Street in 1904. Today this parish of St. Anthony also has a comfortable rectory and a fine modern school.

Rhode Island was another New England state that witnessed the success of the missionaries from Piacenza. Churches were opened in Providence, in Thornton, and in Bristol, interest in religion was fostered, family life and education improved.

If time and space permitted we could go on endlessly giving example after example of dedication to God and neighbor by these men who renounced the joys of home and comfort to labor in the vineyard of the Lord on foreign soil. However, we have to be satisfied with a very few.

Leaving the eastern part of the United States, we continue on to Kansas City, Missouri. The mission there proved to be one of the most difficult. Most of the inhabitants were not Catholics and belonged to a number of different sects and nationalities of many origins, united only in their antipathy toward Catholicism. Moreover, the Italians who had settled there were either wretchedly poor, extremely lazy, or affected by an almost complete indifference toward religion. In consequence, funds and enthusiasm were sadly lacking.

The missionaries had to battle, not only against this situation, but also against an adverse fate. They had been given a church by the bishop, but only temporarily. Later they had built a modest one of their own. On the eve of Easter Sunday of 1903 the usual archenemy struck—fire, and the new church was leveled. The young missionary in charge, awakened by the fire fighters, had barely escaped with his life. He succeeded in saving the Blessed Sacrament, but everything else was lost. The basement of the small mission house had to serve as the church for the time being.

That terrible misfortune had its fortunate side. It stirred up a latent ardor in the hearts of the people. In sorrow at their lost church they drew together to build a new one. Offerings suddenly became more generous. The Church of

Our Lady of the Rosary was inaugurated, and in 1920 the parish celebrated its twenty-fifth anniversary with all debts cleared.

This church had the honor of welcoming a number of illustrious churchmen within its doors. The apostolic delegates, Archbishop Satolli, Archbishop Falconio, Archbishop Bonzano, and the present apostolic delegate, Archbishop Cicognani, were among these. In later years the bishop of Kansas City also entrusted St. John's parish to the Scalabrinians. The latter furnished it with a modern school and built a new chapel as well as a recreational center.

In spite of the many difficulties which arose in its path the parish of Our Lady of the Rosary is still a flourishing one today.

In the state of Ohio the first Scalabrinian mission was founded in Cincinnati. As far back as the middle of the nineteenth century a small group of Italians had settled there. They were good people who led a hard life but who nurtured deep within their hearts the hope that someday they would be able to build their own church and welcome an Italian priest as their pastor. Their high hopes and good intentions always fell short of realization because of what looked like unsurmountable circumstances.

In 1890 two missionaries came from Bishop Scalabrini. In 1893 the church the Italians had dreamed of for so long, almost half a century, was consecrated by the then apostolic delegate, Archbishop Satolli, who dedicated it to the Sacred Heart. In time, following a period of friction, discords, and discouragement, moral and religious progress conquered the opposition.

Columbus, the capital of Ohio, saw the rise of a Scalabrinian mission in the construction of a church dedicated to St. John the Baptist.

In Chicago, Illinois, Archbishop Quigley kept up his interest in the Italian population, in his archdiocese, an interest which he had brought with him from his native Buffalo where he had known and loved his Italian parishioners. He founded several churches for them in the Windy City. In 1903 he sent for the Scalabrinians. In 1904 the Church of the Incoronata, built through their endless efforts, was consecrated. Close on the heels of this church another opened its doors, the Church of St. Michael the Archangel. Nine other parishes were established in Chicago in the years that followed.

CHAPTER 25

Unsung Heroes

. . . the hearts and the
souls of Apostles . . .

THE SAGA OF COURAGE, struggle, and success depicting the
work of the Scalabrinians could go on endlessly, but two
more instances of their irresistible will to help their fellow
men will have to suffice.

Father Peter Bandini founded a colony in Mississippi as
well as in Arkansas. In 1896 a Mr. Austin Corbin, a wealthy
New Yorker and good friend of Prince Ruspoli, then mayor
of Rome, Italy, decided to found a model colony for Italians
at Sunny Side, Mississippi. The prince wrote to Bishop Scalabrini of the project he had in mind and asked for moral support. He suggested that the bishop appoint one of his missionaries to the colony and went so far as to name Father Bandini
as the man of his choice. The suggestion no doubt was made
because of the fact that Mr. Corbin had become acquainted
with Father Bandini and had admired his work for the Italian
immigrants in connection with the St. Raphael Society.

Bishop Scalabrini favored his suggestion, and Father
Bandini accepted the appointment joyfully, since he had
always hoped to see his beloved Italians settle in the country rather than in the crowded city centers. He well knew of
the dangers and temptations confronting the unwary in the
latter.

Sunny Side flourished rapidly and systematically. It had
its own church, a school, as well as a small group of nuns who
would teach the children of the community. Everything

177

seemed to point to a bright future and to an era of prosperity when Mr. Corbin died suddenly and before he had had sufficient time to provide fully and legally for the colony. His heirs did not feel capable or even willing to continue the philanthropic work and leased the project to a group of men whose only interest in it, sad to say, was to make money. As if this were not bad enough, malarial fever broke out, decimating the inhabitants. The others became disillusioned and frightened as well, and many of them migrated to other places. A number of the families, however, clung to Father Bandini, their beloved friend and pastor. They begged him to do something to save their lives and aspirations. During the previous year Father Bandini had spent some months in Arkansas on the advice of his physician. He remembered the healthy climate so suggested going there. The suggestion was gretted enthusiastically. The immigrants from faraway Italy packed up their belongings and started in their search for a new home. This was to be in the Ozarks, in northwestern Arkansas.

Tough times lay before them, but the wanderers were at last able to acquire 800 acres of land, mostly forest. Long-term payments were arranged. The new settlers went to work cutting down trees, building log cabins, making furniture, and tilling the soil.

In mid-spring of 1898 a sudden frost killed the blossoms of every fruit tree, wiping out at one stroke the principal future product of their many labors. A cyclone completed this calamity.

Matters became worse and worse. The neighboring people who looked upon the Italian Catholics with ill-concealed dislike began to perpetrate all kinds of nuisances against them, trying to show them they were not wanted and hoping to drive them away. One final incident brought the matter to a crisis and luckily turned the tide in favor of the Italians. An attempt was made to burn down the school. This was the only stone building of which the settlers could boast, and moreover all their most treasured possessions were stored there.

The incident called for drastic action. The men armed themselves and kept their houses and property well guarded at all times. At the same time Father Bandini appealed to the county judge for protection. The latter proceeded to take efficacious means to secure the safety of the colony and its inhabitants. From that time on peace was established and hostile neighbors became friends.

Victory had crowned the work of strong men and women. Shortly after the new settlers had finished paying for the land for which they had bargained, they increased their holdings, improving and building as they went along. New homes rose, new barns, factories, stores, and schools were opened. Postal and telegraph offices made life less complicated. And most important of all the church was fine enough and large enough to accommodate everyone. It had been placed under the protection of St. Joseph.

Today the old colony bears the name of Tontitown. It was so named in honor of Enrico Tonti, that the memory of the Italian explorer who had been La Salle's companion when the latter explored the Mississippi Valley might not be forgotten.

A former ambassador of Italy to the United States wrote in 1912:

"Father Bandini was the very soul of the colony. He was pastor, notary public, school inspector, postal assistant. He supervised all agricultural efforts, taught Italian, was the leader of the band. . . ."

When Tontitown was inaugurated, the people nominated Father Bandini to be their first mayor. Naturally he did not accept the nomination, but he never ceased to look after the material interests of his people, while at the same time he zealously guarded their spiritual welfare. He was a friend of the governor of Arkansas and was held in affectionate regard by the archbishop of Little Rock.

On January 2, 1917, Father Bandini passed to his reward. A New York paper, *The Italian Herald,* wrote of him thus:

"It may be said that at times Father Bandini may have made mistakes in nurturing ideas that because of his heart burning always with high hopes for his people he held as feasible. In this way unforeseen misfortunes resulted . . . but what cannot be denied is the fact that for his well-loved Italians he made innumerable sacrifices. During his twenty-five years' apostolate among them, he brought wealth to many, smoothed the path for all, yet he himself left this earth so poor that he died alone and penniless in a bare hospital room."

This is to give the fullness of its meaning to the word "missionary!"

Father Bandini was given a solemn funeral in the Cathedral of Little Rock. Bishop Morris himself gave the only eulogy at his humble bier.

Not less edifying is the story of Father Chiariglione, the hero priest of the flying missions, so-called since he was always on the move and had no fixed seat from which to operate. These missions made contact with small groups of immigrants no matter where they were to be found.

Father Chiariglione, a former laborer, soldier, then priest, had finally become a missionary at the age of sixty-five. He began his pilgrimage in 1896 by leaving his parish in Cincinnati and traveling through many a diocese and many a state, visiting localities where Italian families might be alone and left to themselves. He went from house to house as a friend, giving counsel and advice, and interesting himself in their health and in their needs. As a priest of God he baptized their children, regulated marriages, offered the Holy Sacrifice, heard confessions, and distributed Holy Communion.

He visited the old, the sick, and the helpless. He stopped for short or long periods of time wherever and whenever the call came.

In Memphis, Tennessee, he stopped for more than four months that he might be able to pay a visit to each and every one of the families living in the city and its environment. Georgia, Alabama, Florida, all of them saw his gentle presence. At times he found a poor welcome even from his own, but he took it all in stride and never lost heart.

One day he decided to go to Washington from a small town in South Carolina. The distance he had to cover was over 300 miles and he had exactly half a dollar in his pocket. Nevertheless he set out on his journey—on foot. The first night he accepted the hospitality of a Negro who spontaneously offered him shelter on meeting him as he walked alone across the open country. Another night he slept on the steps of a railroad station. Many a night he took his rest in his "beautiful stars hotel," as he called the open field under a canopy of stars.

On reaching a certain town he inquired as to where he could find free lodging for the night. He was directed to a Benedictine monastery, three miles away. His poor old legs had by this time covered twenty miles; three more miles were not too much. He trudged on. Night was fast falling. On reaching his destination he saw two buildings not too far from each other. He had been told that a convent of nuns was also in that vicinity. In the darkness it was hard to decide which was which. A moment of reflective hesitation followed and he made his choice. He rang the bell and waited, trusting to luck. But as luck would have it he had made the wrong choice. The nuns, as can easily be surmised, had sudden qualms about the identity of their nightly visitor. The gate opened slightly and the convent dog rushed out barking. Father stood his ground. Perhaps in surprise at the quiet demeanor of the man he had been sent out to investigate, perhaps for who knows what intuition a dog has, the dog took a friendly attitude. And so it was that a priest and a dog slept that night huddled together near the gate of a convent.

In the morning the monks at the monastery welcomed their guest. Father Chiariglione spent a few days with them and while there learned from a newspaper article that yellow fever had broken out in Montgomery, Alabama. He changed his plan of going to Washington and hastened to the stricken city to offer his services. The bishop was glad for the help and asked Father Chiariglione to care for the sick Italians and French of the city.

When the fever abated, the bishop of Mobile, Alabama, sent for him and placed him in charge of the spiritual welfare of all the Italian and French people scattered throughout the whole of his diocese. This included all of the state of Alabama and part of Florida.

Father Chiariglione was appointed to the town of Daphne, to be used as his general headquarters. In this locality, healthy but poor, lived eighteen families of Italians, some of whom offered to pay him fifty cents each per month for his maintenance. Father Chiariglione refused but accepted whatever food they brought to him. With this and with the small offerings collected at Mass he was satisfied. Each year at Eastertide Italians and Americans united to buy him some new clothes. Two rooms were offered to him free of charge. One he used as his dwelling. There he slept and cooked his simple meals. The other room he turned into a small chapel. The only other church was several miles away and attendance there had taken place only on great holy days. Before his coming the Holy Sacrifice had been offered in Daphne only twice a year.

Father Chiariglione could with justice quote, ". . . *habentes alimenta et quibus tegamur* . . ." [if we have food and clothing to last us out].

From Daphne the good priest traveled many miles to visit

his people, especially at Eastertide. One house after another welcomed him. Everyone knew him and loved him, not only his own, but men and women of different origins, different religions, different color. No wonder that at seventy years of age he was beloved by Americans as well as Europeans, by Negroes as well as whites, by Catholics and Protestants alike! Which all goes to prove that in this world gratitude does exist after all—at least once in a while.

It is told that when Father Chiariglione was telling Bishop Scalabrini of his work the good bishop exclaimed: "Blessed, lucky you!" Perhaps he was regretfully looking back upon the fact that to him it had been denied to live the same life of denial and self-sacrifice which he had so longed for in his youth. But what about the holy joy and the great merit that were his in having inspired love of such a life in the missionaries, a love which had burst forth from his very heart and soul, the heart and the soul of an Apostle of Christ!

CHAPTER 26

Pilgrim for Christ

. . . welcomed by all . . .

IN 1901 the congregation founded by Bishop Scalabrini could boast of fourteen years of apostolic work in North and South America. The time was now ripe for the leader to make a visit of inspection.

The bishop had lived all of his life as a true and faithful father to his flock in the diocese of Piacenza. One by one he had met his sheep in each one of the many parishes scattered throughout its great breadth. For the first time in centuries a bishop had reached out and made close contact with the most remote and inaccessible parishes.

Now the longing in his heart was to meet and know those other sheep that were not of his Piacenza fold, but who had been made his own as it were through his appointed missionaries. He was anxious to form his own opinion of the immigrants' condition by visiting them in person in those lands, to see for himself how much good the congregation that had been born of him had accomplished. He wanted to consider at firsthand the eventual modifications that might be useful and necessary for future work.

Moreover, his missionaries for some time now had been expressing their desire for his visit orally and in numerous letters. The Italians in America, knowing how much they owed him for the moral and material advantages they now enjoyed, enthusiastically clamored for his presence among them, that they might hear his word and express their love and gratitude toward him.

True, the wide ocean lay between, true his diocese took up much of his time and labor, true also the years were beginning to weigh heavily upon him. However, all of these considerations were not in his estimation of sufficient importance to justify renouncing what he felt in conscience to be his bounden duty.

The bishop pondered on the problem from all its angles. And he made his own decisions. In Piacenza now everything seemed to be moving smoothly, his diocese was in a state of tranquillity, a feeling of co-operation was in the air. It was so well organized that it appeared perfectly feasible for the bishop to permit himself an absence of a few months.

The bishops of America had written many letters to the cardinal prefect of propaganda in Rome, telling of their keen desire to welcome their great Italian co-worker whose erudition and spirit of charity they admired, respected, and appreciated so deeply. In consequence, the Sacred Congregation gave its approval for a journey to be undertaken by the bishop and advised him to start as soon as possible.

Bishop Scalabrini immediately went to Rome to see the Holy Father. Pope Leo XIII gave his consent and praised the bishop's intentions, encouraging him in fulfilling his plan, adding his instructions and advice, and, what was so important to the bishop, giving him his blessing.

On July 18, 1901, Bishop Scalabrini sailed from Genoa on the good ship *Liguria*, destined for the port of New York.

As soon as the news of the bishop's journey had become known innumerable telegrams and messages had poured into Piacenza from people of high and low rank everywhere. It was a veritable chorus of approbation and good wishes. Ships of foreign and domestic lines were placed at his disposal. The bishop chose the Italian liner.

The day on which he sailed had all the appearance of a holiday in Genoa. The bishop was accompanied on board by members of the highest authorities, by priests and lay-

men, by relatives and friends, and by the most distinguished
of citizens. The humble lined the streets. The president
of the Italian line, Senator Piaggio, headed the list of well-
wishers.

On board ship there were 1,200 emigrants. How fitting
that the shepherd to the emigrants should be traveling with
them. Thirty cabin passengers were also on board, among
them a Canadian priest, Father Rodier. The latter, on learning that the bishop was alone except for his faithful servant
of many years, offered his services as secretary during the
trip.

In one of the papers of the day we read the following:

"Could there possibly be anyone who refuses to recognize
the real spirit of patriotism of this great bishop, of how utterly devoid he is of any ulterior, selfish motive, of how
completely inspired he is by a deep moral and civic ideal
crowned in Christian splendor? Archbishop Corrigan of New
York City is an invaluable collaborator of our bishop. The
American bishop is an alumnus of Rome where he has nurtured himself on the love of the Catholic Faith and of Italy.
Today this American bishop loves the Italians in his own
land, helps them, and welcomes the Italian priests who go to
America. He has opened schools for our people and is offering great help to the missionaries of Bishop Scalabrini.

"Thinking on these things, we are privileged to offer the
bishop of Piacenza our good wishes for a happy trip in the
name of our paper, the *Cittadino*, and of all Catholic Italians. May these deep-felt good wishes from the citizens of
Italy accompany him in reverence."

The trip across the ocean lasted a little over two weeks.
From the bishop's "diary" we learn that the weather was
pleasant on many a day, damp and far from enjoyable on
others, and that it differed not at all from any other ocean
voyage.

"I eat, drink, sleep, pray, study, meditate. My program is the usual one I follow when at home. I am surrounded by a thousand kindnesses and everyone is most courteous. God through his infinite goodness has always aided me and he has infused into my soul feelings so calm that I hold not even the slightest fear for the future. It is as though I were living my life in my Piacenza study. I bless all of those good people who are praying for their bishop on his journey to the New World."

But the saintly bishop did much more than "eat, drink, sleep, and meditate." From this same diary we see that every afternoon from four to five he taught the children lessons on the catechism, that he offered the Holy Sacrifice each morning, preached to the passengers, heard confessions, distributed Holy Communion, and also confirmed a number of young men.

We read further:

"Today I preached before offering Mass. We are in the middle of the Atlantic. When I happened to mention the motherland, I saw tears. I changed the subject and turned toward our heavenly home. Spirits were lifted. . . . *Vous êtes très éloquent, très imposant,* Father Rodier said to me later. How could anyone keep from being eloquent under such circumstances?"

The *Liguria* reached the port of New York on August 3, 1901.

For an eyewitness account of what had occurred on the morning of the arrival of Bishop Scalabrini we turn to the pages of the *Progresso Italo-Americano,* dated August 4, 1901:

"The arrival of Bishop Scalabrini yesterday was the event of the day. Since the announcement of his coming had been given wide coverage in many of the newspapers of the metropolis and had been acclaimed with such spontaneous expressions of hope and welcome, it could hardly have been otherwise.

"It was six o'clock in the morning when two ferryboats left their piers and started toward Quarantine and there met the *Liguria*. On board were more than 2,000 passengers. Among them were a number of the missionaries of St. Charles, Archbishop Corrigan's secretary, and many distinguished Italians and Americans. There was also an orchestral band, the members of which were from the Abruzzi region of southern Italy.

"The bishop stood on deck waiting for us. At the words of warm and sincere greeting addressed to him a smile touched his lips and his eyes were soft with unshed tears. The band played the Italian anthem and the 'Star-Spangled Banner.' Cheers from the passengers and the immigrants of the *Liguria* mingled with those of the men who had come to meet them. The new arrivals and all those who were present at the ceremony will never be able to erase the day from their memory. It was an unforgettable experience.

"At the New York pier more than sixty carriages were waiting to escort the bishop to the Church of St. Joachim, the church of his missionaries. The streets of the parish were decked out as for a great reception and were jammed with people. As these caught sight of the venerable figure blessing them from his carriage, as they saw him smile telling them without words how happy he was to be among them, they broke out in unrestrained applause."

An American newspaper described it as "almost a royal welcome."

Thousands stood near and around St. Joachim. When the carriage stopped before the doors of the church and the bishop stepped down from the carriage and made his way within the sacred edifice, it was with difficulty that the crowd was restrained from their enthusiasm.

In the church the bishop spoke to the assembled congregation which filled all of the available space. His words were as always warm and sincere. He exhorted his listeners to remain united in spirit with the land of their birth, and at the same time foster respect for themselves and for Italy by obeying the laws and respecting the customs of their new homeland.

Immediately following Benediction, the archbishop of New York came to greet his distinguished guest and to offer to him the hospitality of his episcopal residence. Bishop Scalabrini expressed his gratitude but begged to be allowed to share the humble abode of his missionaries.

In the afternoon he returned the archbishop's visit and their colloquy was most cordial and pleasant. Plans were made for the bishop's sojourn in New York where he was to remain for several weeks.

During these weeks, accompanied by his host, the visiting Italian bishop toured the metropolis, seeing its churches, its schools, its institutes and hospitals, its teeming streets. Not only did he go to the Italian centers, but also to those of other nationalities to see there the splendid progress that had been made by zealous priests and their flocks.

At Ellis Island he assisted at the arrival of hundreds of immigrants from foreign soils and watched with interest the lengthy procedures these hopeful aspirants for American citizenship had to undergo before they were allowed to enter. From these interviews he drew valuable knowledge for future work of advice and assistance. He was given a dinner on the island, after which he was taken on a sight-seeing tour of the neighboring waters aboard one of the island boats.

Let us glance at some of the pages of the bishop's diary for some of the impressions of what he saw:

"On Wednesday, together with Archbishop Corrigan, I visited Ellis Island. We assisted at the arrival of more than 600 Italian immigrants, were present at the examinations and the questionings. Later the chief inspector entertained us at luncheon. Afterwards, he took us on a sight-seeing tour of the port of New York and its surrounding waters. We saw the splendor of the breath-taking panorama offered by this great city and its neighbors as they mirror themselves in the waters of the majestic Hudson. It is an experience that has a somewhat stunning effect. Four million people . . . and all imbued with a restless, feverish activity that knows no limits . . . railroads elevated aboveground . . . wide avenues . . . tall buildings. . . . Here, indeed, new and grandiose ideas are fermenting!"

This was in 1901. What would the good bishop say now of New York City with its almost 9,000,000 inhabitants, its web of subways, its huge piers, its airfields, its skyscrapers, and its population of Italian origin which is larger than that of the capital of Italy! Ideas were truly fermenting, as he put it, at the beginning of the twentieth century!

In New York, Bishop Scalabrini made the acquaintance of Archbishop Ireland of St. Paul, Minnesota. The latter had come to New York to settle a strike and to preside at a labor conference. They exchanged many an opinion and Bishop Scalabrini promised to pay Archbishop Ireland a visit later in the year, a promise fulfilled in late September. We read an account of it in the diary:

"I arrived here from Detroit after twenty-three hours of train ride. The archbishop met me at the station and took me to his residence. St. Paul is a splendid city. A good deal of its population is Italian. Archbishop Ireland has built a stupendous seminary, which accommodates 152 seminarians. The faculty has a staff of distinguished professors. They all speak Italian and French. Yesterday the archbishop invited them for dinner at his residence. It was a truly Italian evening. I felt as though I were entertaining at my residence in Piacenza. One of the professors gave an address in Latin and I answered in the same tongue. The archbishop is a man of great distinction, cultured, zealous, modern, simple in his ways, a man who shows himself as striving solely for the good of souls and the honor of the Church."

A few days after his arrival in New York City Bishop Scalabrini spent almost a week at the Church of Our Lady of Pompei, where he met many of the immigrants who had come from Piacenza. Of his missionaries he had this to say in his diary:

"Our missionaries are doing fine. They are universally well liked and esteemed, and many of the clergy, including Americans, go to them for confession. The bishops are well pleased with them and the work they are doing, and have told me of their keen appreciation of them. They have only one objection. There are not enough of them. How glad I am to have come to these shores and to have seen with my own eyes that notwithstanding some defects in the character of a few of them, their work progresses and they are regarded as real apostles not only by the poor immigrants but also by the hierarchy and the people in general in the United States. May God be praised!"

The bishop paid a visit to Jersey City and to Newark, and in both cities he was acclaimed with great demonstrations of affectionate devotion. In Jersey City the welcome he received looked like a triumphal procession.

A retreat given by Bishop Scalabrini at Dunwoodie, New York, was a great success. Let us go to the diary and read his thoughts on that experience:

"On Monday, August 19, I began to give a retreat at Dunwoodie, New York. The number of missionaries and Italian priests who attended were close to sixty. It was a new and moving experience for me. One of the priests had traveled for two days and two nights, coming as he did from as far away as New Orleans. In fact my listeners had come from almost every state in the Union and represented various regions of Italy. I spoke to them with a deep-seated feeling of genuine emotion and they also seemed greatly touched. On

Sunday, August 25, I addressed them for the last time and at the conclusion we sang the *Te Deum*. We felt as though we were scaling the ladder of heaven. We parted tearfully. Some moments cannot be described."

In Harrisburg, Pennsylvania, he again heard the praises of his missionaries.

"Your missionaries," said the local bishop to him, "are admirable men and we prefer them to all others. They take their shelter wherever they can find it, they live as best they can as long as they can provide for their fellow countrymen. We complain of one thing only. There are not enough of them. All the bishops who have Italians in their dioceses clamor for them."

And again in the diary:

"I, myself, to tell the truth, thought them less well organized, less zealous, and I am overjoyed at their activity and their deep piety. This is of great consolation to me. Defects are not lacking, and in my private talks with them I pointed them out. But these defects are only slight failings in character, in inclinations, in diversities of opinion, all of which do not, in substance, alter the meaning of the apostolic life. I hope that as far as this is concerned my coming will have been of benefit."

In New Haven, Connecticut, the American press, all non-Catholic, described the welcome accorded the bishop by the Italian colony as fantastic.

In Boston, Massachusetts, the reception to the bishop was triumphal. The Italians who at the time numbered about 40,000 went wild in their enthusiasm. There were processions, fireworks, speeches. A group of Irish-American women who cared for young Italian girls were warmly received by the bishop, who was highly impressed by their spiritual goodness and their religious fervor.

The *Italian Herald* had this to say:

"For weeks before the arrival of the Italian bishop from

Piacenza the Italian section of the city under the jurisdiction of the Church of the Sacred Heart was in festive array, as if in readiness for a solemnity more unique than rare."

And the Boston *Herald* wrote:

". . . the whole of the Italian section was hung with bunting and the flags of the United States and Italy. Hundreds and hundreds of lanterns turned the neighborhood into a panorama of light and color. The Church of the Sacred Heart and its square were ablaze with thousands of electric lights . . . a truly edifying scene. A large picture of the bishop, also in lights, dominated the scene. When the parade began to arrive at the square, the crowds were so dense that it was nearly impossible to proceed. No sooner did the police open passage at one spot when another became blocked. Men, women, and children were in the streets, on the balconies, at the windows . . . some, boys of course, had shinnied up the telephone poles and clung precariously to the cross bars. . . ."

The following excerpt in the bishop's diary, dated September 12, is of interest:

"Yesterday I took leave of the archbishop of Boston. The venerable old man told me with great feeling that when he was a young boy he had known all the Catholics in Boston by name, and that they could have been assembled in one large hall. Now he had 600,000 members in his diocese. Today, as I left the church where I had offered the Holy Sacrifice, people I met on the street bade me good-by with tear-filled eyes. . . . To see them so touched and to hear their words of praise was difficult to bear. . . . I hastened to have breakfast and then I was off!"

The same scene took place in Syracuse, Buffalo, Cleveland, Detroit, St. Louis, Cincinnati, Kansas City, and so on and on—the same delirious welcomes, the same affectionate demonstrations, the same praise, the same tribute! What immense, abiding joy and consolation for the shepherd who had traveled so far to meet a flock so far removed from his very own!

On October 10, Bishop Scalabrini arrived in Washington, D.C. He was by then on the homeward leg of his tour of the United States. Theodore Roosevelt, then President of the United States, received him privately at the White House. It is interesting to read of this meeting of two great men as detailed in the bishop's diary:

"Washington! What a marvelous city! It is the finest I have seen so far. I arrived here after a trip which had lasted nineteen hours. Yesterday I visited the apostolic delegate, a man of piety, great prudence, and zeal. This morning at ten o'clock I paid a visit to the President of the United States. He greeted me most kindly as soon as I arrived. Archbishop Ireland had certainly well paved the way for me."

In a conversation he had with the editor of the *Italia Coloniale*, on a later date, the meeting with the President was discussed. The bishop had this to say:

"As soon as we met, the President dismissed two of his cabinet members who were with him at the time. We then spoke on the subject of the Italian immigrants rather at length. The President spoke no Italian, but understood French perfectly. I spoke little English but understood it. The conversation was thus carried on, the President speaking English and I, French. We had no difficulty in getting our thoughts across to each other.

"The President remarked that the Italian immigration is worthy of respect, and that our workers are most necessary where the task at hand is difficult and dangerous, because of their intelligence and because of the efforts they exercise until the task is done. He also added that the Italian laborer certainly does not suffer by comparison with those of other origins."

The two eminent men went on to discuss the Italian immigrant from the point of view of his standing in the opinion of the American people. It was brought out that the children as a whole did well in school, that in crime, when considered from the general whole, the Italians were not worse than others.

We refer again to the bishop's own words:

"When I mentioned two cases of crime in Detroit, the President cut in with: 'Stabbing, probably.' I replied that I could not say, but I tried to point out that although I deplored the fact of the crimes being committed, and although I realized that all possible remedies must be applied to cure this situation, I felt that we should agree that this state of affairs had to a great extent been brought about by the fact that the Italians had felt themselves despised and often ridiculed. I remarked that often accused unjustly, and goaded and aroused at times beyond their endurance by the insults flung at them, they struck back in self-defense. I cited an incident of which I had been an eyewitness at Ellis Island just a few weeks before. At Ellis Island I had seen a guard strike an immigrant across the legs as if he had been an animal and not a man. The blow had been dealt by one who was supposed to uphold the law and protect it. The immigrant had turned against his tormentor and had slapped him soundly, adding the remark that it was luck he had no weapon handy. I admitted to the President that the man had done wrong in lifting up his hand against a duly-elected officer of the law, but, I inquired, did the President consider it correct for that officer to treat a humble immigrant in such a way? The President deplored the occurrence and assured me that the Italians had his entire sympathy."

The whole of the conversation had been most cordial and had lasted more than an hour. At its conclusion Mr. Roosevelt had highly praised the work done by the Scalabrinians and had wished them all success, promising every help by himself and his government.

From Washington the bishop went on to Baltimore, where he spent a whole day with James Cardinal Gibbons. The two prominent churchmen, so easy of manner, so affable in their gentleness, so humble in their wisdom, were immediate friends. As the bishop said later, when speaking of his meeting with Cardinal Gibbons, "we parted as friends of long standing."

CHAPTER 27

Prophetic Farewell

---

*. . . When all voices, be they in different
tongues, will be lifted up in one great hymn
of praise to the Almighty . . . America . . .
the Promised Land . . . will definitely
assume the leadership of the world . . .*

NEW YORK again welcomed Bishop Scalabrini, when he returned to the metropolis on October 12, at the close of a journey which had covered more than 9,000 miles. The trip had been an eventful one in many respects. The bishop had met and spoken with many personalities of the day, all of whom had praised him and had shown affectionate regard toward him. Moreover, the journey had been pleasant, had run smoothly, and had been untouched by inconveniences of any sort whatever.

In the great metropolis he continued his visits and continued to gather information from the people he met and the places he saw. In the future this information was to be of the greatest value to him in his work for the Italian immigrants.

The time was drawing close for his return to Italy. But one more reception of note was to be given for him. The famous Catholic Club of New York, in its admiration for the great foreign prelate, opened its doors to him in solemn reception on October 15. It was perhaps the finest that had been given in his honor.

We refer to the *Italian Herald* for a lucid account of the brilliant affair:

"The Catholic Club of New York is among the wealthiest and most honored and influential clubs of the metropolis. It has a membership of almost 1,500 persons, among whom are the names of millionaires, magistrates, judges, professional men, army and navy officers, congressmen, and others of national prominence.

"Any reception within its walls is a social event in which the press shows as much interest as in social functions of the renowned 'four hundred.' The fame of its hospitality in and outside New York is second to none.

"The fact that this club honored Bishop Scalabrini with so brilliant a reception should be made known to the Italians here and abroad. Perhaps more than an expression of admiration for the bishop of Piacenza it was from start to finish a hymn of hope for a closer union between Italians and Americans. It was as a defense of our immigration for those who do not know it, those who know it only superficially, those who fail to acknowledge it through prejudice.

"At 9:00 P.M. the orchestra intoned a triumphal march as Bishop Scalabrini and Archbishop Corrigan, accompanied by high church dignitaries, by the president of the club, and by many distinguished citizens, made their entrance into the magnificent gold-and-white reception hall. It was a stirring sight, dignified and imposing.

"The guest of the day took the seat of honor on the dais at one end of the hall. The others sat on either side of him.

"The president of the club introduced the guest of honor with words of warm praise and admiration. He addressed him as the indefatigable apostle of his people and called upon others to express the common sentiments of devotion for him and his cause.

"Mr. Paul Muller, a distinguished lawyer, spoke in French and was equal to his task. Every paper should feel in duty bound to print his talk in full and diffuse it and comment upon it throughout the nation. Special attention should be given to what we consider to be its most important part. This deals with the question of the Italian immigrants, and stresses the point of the necessity for a better evaluation both of them and of the problems with which they are confronted. It also gives voice to the future that should await them in a brotherly acknowledgment of the good qualities they possess.

"Bishop Scalabrini followed Mr. Muller and also spoke in French. He delivered his address without referring for an instant to any notes prepared in advance, so that his message seemed to be pouring out of the depths of his heart, as if inspired. He held his audience in a spell with the mastery of his oratory, vibrant with faith and hope, especially when he envisioned America as the promised land of humanity and of the religion of Christ. His words were a luminous proof of a superior mind and a magnanimous heart before which even those who might be found wanting in religious fervor bow in reverence as before a master.

"The archbishop of New York was the last speaker and his words of appreciation for his august guest and friend were warmly applauded."

We feel that we cannot neglect giving the most salient points of that memorable address:

"America," said Bishop Scalabrini, "and I say this with heartfelt emotion, is the land bequeathed to the world by Our Lord Jesus Christ, the Promised Land of the Catholic Church.

"Here someday, if quiescence and self-satisfaction, ignorance of the ways pointed out by God Almighty, and opposition to holy inspirations do not lead people astray from the divine plan, all of the national groups present within this fortunate land will bring forth numerous, rich, contented, moral, and religious generations which, although clinging still to their own national characteristics, will be closely knit together into one integral whole.

"From this land of unbounded blessings will come forth great inspirations; new forces will radiate; these inspirations and forces will regenerate and give new life to this old world by teaching it the true concept of liberty, brotherhood, and equality. The Old World will be shown how people of many diverse origins can be united politically and spiritually, without the necessity of barriers rising up to impoverish or destroy anyone, and yet at the same time still fondly remember their native tongues, their own ethnological characteristics.

"Thus for America and through America will the great promise of the Gospels be fulfilled, and there shall be but one fold and one shepherd.

"The supreme goal prefixed by Divine Providence for the human race is not the conquest of material things through more or less progressive science. It is not the molding of great nations within which hour by hour the genius of power, knowledge, and wealth is developed and realized. No, indeed. It is rather by far the union of the souls of men in God through His Divine Son, Our Lord Jesus Christ, and through His visible representative here on earth, the Roman Pontiff. The obstacles which are still opposing the will and the designs of God Almighty will be leveled one by one. There will come a day, a day the dawn of which will first be seen in this great and glorious America, wherein the nations of the world will recognize where real, genuine greatness is to be found. On that day these nations will realize the dire need of returning to their Father's house . . . and they will return!

"I am hoping for this, gentlemen. Today the world is in a state of turmoil, blinded by its own prosperity, its own progress. Man feels exalted by his conquest over matter and lords it over nature as its master, tearing the lifeblood out of its soil, taming the lightning, bringing confusion among the waters of the ocean. Distances are being wiped out. Nations fall, rise, and renew themselves once more. Races reach out and intermingle. Through the noise and the clatter of our machines, beyond all this feverish activity of work, in the upsurge of these gigantic achievements, a far vaster, far more noble and sublime plan is maturing. This is the union of all people under God.

"What a triumphant day that will be, gentlemen! A joyous day, when all voices, be they in many different tongues, will be lifted up in one single hymn of praise to the Almighty! The sun of truth will then pour itself upon the world in a great brilliance and the rainbow of peace, as has been said by an illustrious Italian, will enfold the world in all of its tender colors. It will be as an arch of triumph. Society, once more bound together in the Christian spirit, will continue on its way, orderly, just, treading the path of true liberty, civilization, and prosperity.

"Finally, gentlemen, with the assurance that this day will be one of the fondest memories of my life, I give you deepest thanks, for myself and for my co-nationals. May God bless you and reward you and your dear friends!"

Bishop Scalabrini was not trying to expound beautiful rhetoric. In his words he was only attempting to bring together the ideas he had expressed on many other occasions. Hence his meaning must be considered as part of his interpretation of the modern evolution of history. A brief analysis of his thoughts will highlight both the man and his work.

He was one of the first to foresee that America would one day be the "Promised Land of the Catholic Church." He foretold this at a time when Catholics in America formed one seventh of the whole population, and most of them belonged to the poorer classes. Few indeed were the Catholics who then held conspicuous positions in the political or administrative life of the land. The Catholic Church was far from possessing the vast and splendid organization of today in the strictly religious or in the social and educational fields.

In his travels Bishop Scalabrini had envisioned the glorious destiny which was in the offing for the United States. He felt the peaceful, contented assimilation which was taking place among the various national groups of immigrants. With crystal-clear insight he perceived a happy co-existence that would demonstrate, perhaps, the possibility even of a system of political union for the various nations of Europe. This idea he justly stressed, in spite of the fact that at that very time a number of native organizations were beginning to gain strength, groups of people who were raising doubts as to the possible assimilation of certain minority groups, and fomenting those prejudices which in later years were to bring about discriminatory laws on immigration.

The bishop understood the wholesome principles and tendencies at the root of American culture. In them he saw the seed that was destined to give the Old World a renewal of life. It was his keen intuition that made him realize that the United States would place itself at the head of a peaceful revolution that would bring the nations of Europe together to carry them forward toward economic and social co-operation, which eventually would mean political unity in a spirit of liberty.

And this great visionary portrayed such a picture at a time when the Monroe Doctrine was a veritable dogma in the minds of the people, and when no one would have dared even to suspect that on a day in the not-too-distant future America would not only abandon its isolationism, but would definitely assume leadership in the world.

He showed no hesitation in maintaining that the great hopes placed in the technical progress of modern civilization would vanish, and that the people of the United States would be the first to feel the need for a return to spiritual values and to that integral Christianity which has as its head the Vicar of Christ on earth. Today, in the United States, encouraging signs of such a back-to-God necessity appear clearer than anywhere else in the world.

The foresight shown by the great bishop of Piacenza a half century ago is indeed amazing. Indeed, his over-all vision of events and developments still so far away in time, so far that such events were not even dreamed of by Americans themselves, holds an intangible quality of prophecy. One fact emerges clear and distinct as to the reason why Bishop Scalabrini not only championed immigration valiantly and courageously when faced with almost insurmountable odds, but also appraised it at its just value, that is, as a phenomenon of the highest social value. In the very movement of people from one land to another, in the melting together of old and new cultures, he foresaw and awaited a great and wholesome rebirth, hopeful and salutary. This was the impulse which spurred him on. This is what urged him to struggle on to have the immigrants recognized as worthy of respect and love, to have them appreciated, cared for, taught, and assisted.

Such an achievement was for him the fulfillment of the highest goals, which might in time bring about well-being, happiness, and success throughout the world, seething so restlessly in the throes of a tragic crisis; a crisis born of and steeped in the social upheaval brought about and set afoot by secularism.

Bishop Scalabrini's visit to the United States ended on November 12, 1901, when he sailed back to Italy.

We could write many more pages telling of his triumphs, but we find it necessary to restrain ourselves.

Let us sum up by giving our readers an excerpt from a letter written by a missionary of St. Charles who was himself a native of Piacenza:

"Bishop Scalabrini stopped in the United States for a period of three months and five days. In that brief time he gave 345 sermons, bestowed the sacrament of Confirmation upon hundreds of people, traveled night and day, covering thousands of miles. He slept on trains, withstood changes of diet, climate, habits. And yet in the midst of such a heavy schedule he was always seen as serene and contented. Thank God he always enjoyed the best of health during the entire period he stayed here. This is an evident sign that God wanted him in the United States to do much good for the Italians who had migrated here. And he certainly succeeded.

"We must indeed be grateful to God, since this short stay by him has raised high the moral status of the Italians in general. All without exception have recognized him as a saintly man and as an Apostle.

"His coming was a great consolation for us, his departure is a bitter experience. His presence, his example, a single word from his lips, shed light and courage upon the most arduous of enterprises as well as upon the most difficult task. What a privilege it is for the people of Piacenza to have so holy a bishop, one who is truly a glory of the episcopate. . . ."

This epitomizes the feelings of all those who had the great fortune of knowing him.

On November 26 the bishop arrived at Naples. On the twenty-ninth he was received by Pope Leo XIII. On December 1, he was in conference with the Italian minister for foreign affairs. And at last, on December 4, his holy mission accomplished, he returned to his Piacenza where his flock gave him a delirious welcome.

CHAPTER 28

Off to South America

. . . from South America
came a cry for help . . .

No sooner had Bilshop Scalabrini returned to his native Italy than rumors began to be circulated that before long he would sail away again across the Atlantic. "This time he will go to South America," many who knew him kept repeating.

The bishop did not affirm or deny the rumors. To anyone who sought information on the subject he would give an evasive answer. "I cannot tell," he would say in a faraway manner, "for, after all, I do have to square accounts with my birth certificate. It states that I am sixty-two years old. Who knows?"

His age was not the only obstacle. For a period of time he had been far from wholly well. In fact, the illness about which he spoke to no one was to cause his death in the not-too-distant future.

In the mind of the bishop who had always been a missionary at heart there lingered the vision of what he had seen on the North American continent. From his trip he had accumulated a world of information and hence had drawn such pertinent conclusions that now he was more than ever fully convinced that the difference is very great indeed between what is gained through personal experience and what is learned by mere hearsay. He had visited faraway places and made contact with his distant missionaries. Thus he now had a much clearer perspective of the intellectual and moral

qualities that were to be considered as an absolute necessity in these men if they were to carry out their work successfully on foreign soil.

He had been to North America, he could truly say he
knew what was going on there, but what about South America? He had been told and had read of how different were
conditions there from the northern continent. He knew as
a natural consequence that the remedies to be applied there
must be different. He was in constant touch with his missionaries in South America by frequent interchange of cor-
respondence, but he was far from satisfied. Up to that time
he had not been able to form a clear concept of the situation.
Hence, in spite of age or infirmities, he knew that nothing
should prevent him from leaving his diocese once again, to
see what he could do to help the work of his missionaries.

Two years after his return from North America he made it
known that he had decided to go to Brazil. He had come to
his decision after long and deep thinking and against the advice of many. His own brother who lived in Brazil and was
well aware of all the difficulties and hardships the bishop
would encounter joined his friends in begging and arguing
against the venture, but to no avail.

Years before, in 1887 to be exact, when Bishop Scalabrini
had written his well-known pamphlet *The Italian Immigration to America,* a writer for the French paper *L'Observa-
teur Français* of August 5, 1887, had written articles which
had greatly stirred the bishop of Piacenza. No doubt its content had left a profound impression on his mind and had led
to his decision. This is part of what he had read:

". . . In Brazil and in other countries of South America
it is the emissaries of the Freemasons who work to inoculate
the poison of indifferentism and even worse evils into minds
and souls of those who are today completely without religious comforts or assistance. At the center of an immense

territory which extends from Panama to Cape Horn many of the Italian immigrants live in the midst of endless forest or on the slopes of the Cordilleras. There they have no communication with the civilized world. Little by little they adopt the customs of the savages, losing all remembrance of their native land, its customs and its ideas. The religion of their fathers fades away. Finally they end up in a primitive state of life that is almost brutish in its concept, and barely distinguishable from the indigenous populations who have never known Christianity, nor any form of civilization.

"An Italian explorer went from one end to the other of this vast territory. With deep emotion and horror at the same time he tells of having met a great number of Italians in the forests and mountains of South America. He describes them as having been reduced to the state of savages, naked and wild. He said they seemed to have completely forgotten their origin, although they still spoke their native dialects.

"Another told of meeting numerous Italian families and on speaking with them they had described the loneliness and misery of their lives and how they felt themselves forgotten and abandoned by their own. They had begged him with touching words to plead with their bishops of old and their priests as soon as he would return to Italy. When these poor peasants spoke of their little village churches, of the priests they had left behind, of the Mass and Benediction, of the nostalgic sound of the church bells, of the sacred hymns they had never heard again, of the Sacraments they could no longer approach, they had wept bitterly. He who had been present at such scenes felt they were etched on his brain with letters of fire.

"These recitals by eyewitnesses and the reports sent by American bishops on the ravages brought about by force and circumstance to these wretched immigrants are the fundamental reasons which have led the bishop of Piacenza to make himself the promoter of a needed movement that at one and the same time will contribute to their well-being and eternal salvation.

"It is the love of neighbor in his heart, his veritable passion for the salvation of abandoned souls, exposed to endless attacks and dangers, that urges him on. . . ."

What happened in South America from the time the Scalabrinian missionaries had gone there has an aura of the unbelievable. If in North America it may be said that these men could be called builders and molders of citizens, in South America it can be said that they were real pioneers in the sense that they brought civilization where there was literally none. They were the ones who encouraged and aided those who had dared to face the unknown dangers of the jungles and the forests never before trod by white settlers. They were the ones who took it upon themselves to turn bare, endless prairies into fertile fields by walking along with the tiller and the builder, with indomitable courage and faith.

At the beginning of the twentieth century the number of Italian immigrants in the southern part of Brazil was close to the one million mark. Many of them were tillers of the soil in the *fazendas*, the coffee plantations. Others had been given temporary grants of land by the government. The land was to be theirs after a certain period of years, that is when the necessary improvements had been made and the stipulated price paid. Some of them had been successful, others had been forced to give up the struggle and choose other means for survival. Often life became a nightmare. It was not easy for them to accustom themselves to it and its demands.

Those who overcame all obstacles finally did obtain material success, but from the moral and spiritual point of view things went from bad to worse. A good priest here and there, dedicated and energetic, had tried his best to surmount the insurmountable, but long distances and the absence of roads made the task almost impossible.

Then the Scalabrinians came. With an utter disregard of difficulties, big or little, they faced the situation squarely, and prepared for any eventuality that might arise to prevent what they had made up their minds to do.

God must have walked with them. In 1904, means of communication in Brazil were still barely existent. Bishop Scalabrini had been told all this by his brother, and told that therefore the contemplated trip was unwise. All efforts to dissuade him, as we know, came to naught. His missionaries had gone there when things were much worse. He had said he would go, and so go he would.

Early in 1904 he set about making himself ready. He didn't know Portuguese. Undaunted, he went to work and learned it. So well, in fact, that in a few months he understood and spoke it fluently. This is attested to by the man who taught him the language, Professor Motti, and by those who heard him give talks extemporaneously in Brazil.

On June 13, 1904, he left Piacenza. He had made his last will and all arrangements for the proper functioning of the work of his diocese during his absence. His great wish had been to slip away quietly, without fuss or fanfare. He wanted no demonstrations to take place at his departure. However, his flock refused to let him go without showing their pride in him. A crowd was waiting at the station. Priests, men and women of noble rank, and simple, everyday folk were all there, to acclaim him and wish him Godspeed, success, and a safe return. Bishop Bonomelli, his old friend, came all the way from Cremona to see him off.

The bishop was accompanied by six missionaries and his faithful old servant who had gone with him on his first trip. At Genoa a group of Sisters were to board the same ship on which he was to travel.

On June 14 he was given a private audience by St. Pius X. The audience was lengthy, and at its conclusion Bishop Scalabrini felt encouraged and satisfied that in going to South America he was fulfilling a wish that had been expressed by St. Pius X many times.

On June 18 the bishop sailed from Naples on the *City of Genoa*. On the preceding day he had written the following words in his diary:

"Today I can say that our mission has begun. I shall go on from here, certain of success, relying on the manifold powers granted me by the Holy Father."

The long trip to the South American continent took almost three weeks, and it was anything but pleasant as far as the weather was concerned. From the very start it looked as if the warnings of hard times that had been given the bishop were coming true.

At first the sea was calm, the air cool. As the ship neared the equator, however, the heat gradually became almost unbearable. There were no air-conditioners then and the inside of the ship became an immense oven. The sea also added to the general discomfort, gray as the sky overhead, rough, turbulent. Calm periods, when not a breath of air came to relieve the suffering, were followed by sudden battering storms. Later, after they passed the equator, a cold, blustering wind rose. The sun shone, but walking on deck was impossible. One of the crew members was severely injured. To make matters worse, a quarrel broke out between an Italian and an Arab. A panic almost ensued. Calm returned only because of the quick thinking of the captain.

On July 3 a terrible storm struck. Throughout the night the fury of the storm rose to such a pitch that the passengers were terrorized. But by morning all was well.

During the whole trip the bishop felt no discomfort, a remarkable fact considering his age. He wrote in his diary:

"I, as always, insist on being healthy. It is God who in spite of my great unworthiness takes good care of his servant. How grateful I am! I am here for Him, and for Him I shall fulfill my task, one which has been inspired in me by Him, even though it may mean the sacrifice of my life. . . ."

His days, like those of his former trip, were far from idle. The passengers were his flock. They needed his ministrations and he was as ready as always to serve God through his neighbor.

July 7 and Rio de Janeiro!

We read in the diary of July 6:

"Friend Wind certainly likes us . . . it is still with us. God willing we shall be in Rio tonight and tomorrow morning we shall set foot on Brazilian soil.

"The first lap of my journey is thus happily concluded. And now, not without regret, I must put a stop to my writing of these notes. Somehow, as I did it, I had the momentary feeling that I was back in my study in Piacenza or in our little garden . . . among my beloved flock . . . and to think that I am so many thousands of miles away!

"In my thoughts I am hastening my return. I hope I shall be home by November 1. And yet, always and in all things, may God's will be done."

In Rio de Janeiro the local bishop, a great number of religious and priests, and a huge crowd of people greeted Bishop Scalabrini on his arrival.

In the city of São Paulo a third of the population were Italians. There the bishop was glad to see that his missionaries enjoyed the respect and the love of their people. On visiting the two orphan asylums founded by them, capable of housing 200 orphans, he realized the reason for the praises heaped upon them.

About two hundred miles from São Paulo he heard of the

owner of a coffee plantation, a good Catholic who had built a small church for the benefit of his workers.

"Oh, if only I had one hundred zealous priests at my disposal," he exclaimed, "God's glory in this land would be so great, and so much good could be done for these abandoned souls—almost a million of them!"

From São Paulo he sailed to the State of Paraná, landing at Paránaguá. From here he went by train to Curitiba, the capital of the state, where he was received with open arms by both religious and civic authorities. Just as in North America he was invited to stay where he would be comfortable and honored, but again he chose to dwell in the humble abodes of his missionaries.

In the beautiful city of Porto Alegre the bishop stopped for a rest. It lasted two days! On September 12 he began the most difficult and arduous part of his journey. The only way of reaching his destination was on horseback. This meant he had to undergo excruciating physical pain, affected as he was with hydrocele. He endured it for seven full hours.

The little town of Encantado was waiting for him. People from the nearby mountains, hills, and forests had left their huts and their burrows and poured into the village to see and hear the famous pilgrim from Italy. It was crowded to capacity.

Bishop Scalabrini remained there for ten days, for he found there was much work laid out for him. Hundreds had to be confirmed, hundreds advised and encouraged, and just before he took his leave he consecrated the Church of St. Peter.

From Encantado he rode on to other towns and villages, never sparing himself for the sake of those who needed his encouraging presence and word. In one place, Capoeiras, he found he had to confirm 1,500.

His journey through the colonies of the Rio Grande lasted five weeks. During that period he administered the sacrament of Confirmation to 15,000 persons. This, added to all else he did, was truly remarkable, for it is hard to believe when one considers the obstacles that had to be overcome. But he never seemed weary, the kindness of his smile was never lessened. It was the fortitude, the smile of joy of the apostle who regrets only one thing—to be able to do so "very" little, as he thought.

Brazil was left behind and Buenos Aires was next on the bishop's itinerary. In Buenos Aires he had the great comfort of seeing his brother Professor Peter Scalabrini. They had not seen each other in forty years!

The Salesian Fathers had been given orders by their superior general to receive him at their institute as if he were their superior general himself, but the bishop preferred to spend two days of domestic tranquillity with his own brother. It seemed to him that this visit was a gift from God himself, and he wanted to accept it in all humility and enjoy it.

On November 11 he sailed back to Italy and arrived in Genoa on December 5.

Pope St. Pius X wrote, congratulating him on the amount of good he had done and expressing his desire of hearing from his own lips the details of the trip. From this talk and others which the bishop had with various ecclesiastics, results ensued which reached into the future even to the present day.

The problems of both North and South America were discussed, remedies suggested which were far from simple but feasible for men of courage and determination. Bishop Scalabrini had willed to see his ideas put to the test and had fulfilled them himself to a great extent. He set to work and wrote voluminously of his ideas and plans to the Sacred Congregation for the Propagation of the Faith and to the cardinal secretary of state of the Holy See. His last message is dated May 17, 1905, two weeks before his death.

Yes, men do pass away, but their ideas, if truly noble and

worthy, never die. Rather, because of their salutary weight, they impress themselves, grow and bring fruit wherever they have fallen.

Seven years later St. Pius X published a *Motu Proprio*. It dealt with the emigration of Catholics to foreign lands and announced the founding within the Sacred Consistorial Congregation of a new department whose purpose was to care for the spiritual needs of these emigrants and to regulate all that concerned them.

Benedict XV, successor to St. Pius X, later still inaugurated the Pontifical Institute for Emigration and an emigration prelate was appointed as its director.

This was one further step in the organization visualized and hoped for by Bishop Scalabrini for so many years.

CHAPTER 29

Bishop Scalabrini Points Out the Way
to Mother Cabrini

. . . two great souls . . . two great minds
. . . two workers of miracles . . .

THE LOMBARD PRIEST who in later years was to become
bishop of Piacenza, the man who had worked with un-
remitting zeal and relentless energy, had triumphed over the
lashings of fate and the enmity of men. People of all classes
were now following his suggestions and his example. Under
his constant inspiring and vigilant tutelage they were able to
give form and reality and force through the years to what
had been born of charity and humility.

Three congregations of Sisters also owe much of their present spirit and development to Bishop Scalabrini's leadership.

The first of these to come in contact with the Servant of
God were Mother Cabrini and her daughters.

Mother Frances Xavier Cabrini, like Scalabrini, was also a
daughter of Lombardy and from childhood had held in her
heart the longing to be a missionary. She had founded the
Missionary Sisters of the Sacred Heart and hoped that a time
would come when she would find the way of going to the
Orient, there to gain souls for Christ, as her patron saint, St.
Francis Xavier, had done. But God had other plans for her.

Bishop Scalabrini was the first to suggest that she go to
America. He knew and understood what wonders this inspired soul would perform in the interest of the Italian
immigrants in the New World. She was reluctant to follow

215

his advice. One city, New York, one country, the United States, was not that too small a task to satisfy the call in her soul to gain souls for Christ?

Bishop Scalabrini sought to persuade her to accept his suggestion. He told her of the wretched, soul-thirsty Italians in the United States for whom a woman's hand, a woman's comforting words, would mean a rebirth and a regeneration. Frances Cabrini listened, but she was still averse to giving up her dream. Besides, she wanted her nuns to go out as missionaries, yes, but independent of others. She did not like the idea of being too exclusively associated with the work of the Scalabrinian Fathers. And she bided her time.

Bishop Scalabrini, however, was not easily put off. He also waited, but in the meantime he placed his ideas before Leo XIII and wrote to Archbishop Corrigan of New York of the immense zeal and brilliant ability of Mother Cabrini, suggesting that he send her an invitation to go to New York. He had realized that Mother Cabrini was a practical woman and that he might be able to persuade her to accept his views if he had something concrete to present to her.

A letter from Archbishop Corrigan reached Mother Cabrini, but she remained doubtful as to the advisability of going to the United States. She decided to consult the Pope himself.

In December 1888 Mother Cabrini left Codogno for Rome. Bishop Scalabrini, who in the meantime had written to Archbishop Corrigan asking for a more decisive letter, had also gone to Rome. He had the firm intention of asking the Sacred Congregation for the Propagation of the Faith and the Pope that a group of nuns be sent among the Italians of New York. He again suggested that Mother Cabrini, who was still seeking a mission field for her labors, be sent to the United States.

During her first audience with Leo XIII Mother Cabrini

did not refer to the subject of America, since no answer had as yet arrived from Archbishop Corrigan.

At this time Bishop Scalabrini was pressing Mother Cabrini for a definite answer to his request.

Mother Cabrini ever since her childhood had relied on prayer and inspiration. At moments of crisis dreams had come to her, as though to point out the way her decisions should take. It happened that in this situation she decided to begin a novena. Before she finished it the usual dream came. In it she saw her mother among a group of saints and she heard her urging her to go to America. She was also told that on the following day she would get the letter from the archbishop of New York.

The next morning, on her way to the Vatican, she met Bishop Scalabrini and told him about her dream. The Servant of God looked at her and laughed:

"You and your dreams!" he said.

But Mother Cabrini must have laughed, too, when she received him that afternoon and he held out a letter to her. It was from New York.

"Archbishop Corrigan has written," he said. "Now get ready to go."

Mother Cabrini was still not completely won over. One person alone could dispel her doubts—the Pope—Pope Leo XIII! She went to him.

The Pope listened to her arguments as she knelt before him. He must have wondered how so frail and diminutive a woman could house so boundless a spirit. As she finished, he gave her his answer:

"Not to the East, Cabrini, but to the West!"

The Head of the Church had spoken. There was no more hesitation on her part. And, incidentally, Bishop Scalabrini had won.

In January 1889 Bishop Scalabrini had the joy and the

satisfaction of being able to inform Archbishop Corrigan that Mother Cabrini and the Sisters had decided to go to New York.

On March 19, 1889, in the chapel of the mother house of the Missionaries of the Sacred Heart at Codogno, Bishop Scalabrini happily bestowed his blessing upon Mother Cabrini and six of her Sisters, offering to each of them the crucifix of the missionary. They carried these to America with them. It was most fitting that Bishop Scalabrini should preside over the departure ceremony for, as Pius XII says in the Apostolic Constitution *Exul Familia*, it was especially because of his advice and encouragement that Mother Cabrini made her final decision to go to the United States and undertake her American enterprise.

In New York the beginnings were very hard for Mother Cabrini and her Sisters, even harder than she had foreseen. Archbishop Corrigan had certainly not expected them to arrive as early as the end of March. Mother Cabrini had written to him on February 16, to say that she had the intention of sailing in May, if not "sooner," but the end of March was indeed much "sooner." Moreover, just at that time Archbishop Corrigan and Countess Cesnola, who was supposed to arrange for the establishment of the new nuns in an orphanage for Italian girls, were unfortunately having a serious disagreement.

Nor could the Scalabrinian Fathers be of much help to them, pressed as they were at the moment by serious financial difficulties. They themselves had arrived in New York only the year before, and had just purchased an old Protestant church which had been adapted for Catholic worship. This had meant the incurring of a large debt. They had no rectory as yet, and were living in a few rented rooms. Their condition in general was as poor as that of the Italian immigrants they had come to help and to whose mentality they had to adapt themselves, at least at the beginning of their efforts.

Mother Cabrini, however, was not to be daunted, and with her firmness and faith she overcame all obstacles. On her trip to Italy, three months later, she was able to report to Bishop Scalabrini that her Sisters had already gathered together 400 little Italian girls in the orphanage, and that they were also operating an Italian school for the Scalabrinian Fathers, which was connected with the parish of St. Joachim.

From that day on Mother Cabrini's conquests knew no limits. The eastern part of the United States, the West, the North, and the South, all benefited by her zeal and her energy, and most of all by her unswerving faith. She had come to the United States penniless and unknown, yet she built schools, hospitals, institutes, all of which sprang up as if by magic. In South America the story of what she had achieved in the United States was repeated over and over again, bringing consolation and regeneration to thousands of Italian immigrants.

The hopes placed in Mother Cabrini by the bishop of Piacenza had been fully realized, perhaps even beyond his vision of them. Divine Providence had used the "Father to the Italian Immigrants" in a most admirable way to present them with an incomparable "Mother."

More closely connected with the Scalabrinian Fathers' work, however, were two other congregations of Sisters, known by several different names in the two Americas.

Bishop Scalabrini had long foreseen the need of a group of Sisters dedicated primarily to the assistance of the Italian immigrants and ready to adapt themselves to the particular circumstances in which the Italians found themselves living. Besides, his missionaries had asked him more than once to complete his undertakings on behalf of these immigrants by founding an order of Scalabrinian nuns. It was with the idea of extending his work that Bishop Scalabrini welcomed the opportunity offered to him by Divine Providence of doing something along this line.

One opportunity presented itself in the fall of 1895, due to the initiative of that dynamic priest, Father Joseph Marchetti. Father Marchetti, sent by Bishop Scalabrini to Brazil in 1895, had founded an orphanage there and had returned to Italy that same year in order to found a group of nuns who would be willing to take care of the children of the orphanage. After discussing the matter with Bishop Scalabrini, Father Marchetti went to his native Lucca and there recruited three young women who were thinking of dedicating themselves to the religious life. Among them was Father Marchetti's own sister. His mother, Carolina Marchetti, then a widow, decided to follow her two children and consecrate herself to the service of Christ. They all went to Piacenza, where Bishop Scalabrini gave them the warmest of welcomes. They resided for a time at the Institute for the Deaf and Dumb, which the Servant of God had founded some years before. On October 25, 1895, Bishop Scalabrini offered a special Mass for them in his private chapel, and received their semi-public vows of poverty, chastity, and obedience, to be binding for a period of six months.

Normally, a period of postulancy and a canonical year of novitiate must precede the admission of candidates to the religious profession. The need for the care of the São Paulo orphanage was so urgent, however, that Bishop Scalabrini had decided that the four postulants should make their novitiate and their perpetual vows in São Paulo. For the time being the vows given into his hands for six months would be a sufficient guarantee for the unity and the perseverance of the four postulants.

Bishop Scalabrini gave Father Marchetti a manuscript copy of the rules and regulations he had prepared for the new order and instructed him to make all the changes he would deem necessary in order to adapt them to the kind of life the Sisters would be leading and dealing with in São Paulo. Father Marchetti was then to submit them to him for final approval.

Moreover, Bishop Scalabrini authorized Father Marchetti to accept new postulants, admit them to the novitiate, and accept their vows.

On October 27, 1895, the new Sisters, accompanied by Father Marchetti, left Piacenza and headed for Brazil, which was to become their first and chief field of activity.

These were the humble beginnings of the Missionary Sisters of St. Charles. God blessed them and their work, and today they have four novitiates in Italy, the United States, and Brazil. They conduct three homes for the aged, twenty elementary schools, seven high schools, and twenty hospitals. In Brazil and in Europe as well they nurse patients in their own homes. They do domestic work in almost all of the seminaries conducted by the Scalabrinian Fathers and are of great help in many of their mission centers.

Bishop Scalabrini is venerated also as the cofounder of the Missionary Zelatrices of the Sacred Heart. These Sisters were founded by a saintly and wealthy girl, Clelia Merloni, in Viareggio, Italy, in 1894. But the new religious institution soon found itself facing obstacles that threatened its very existence. Because of the shady manipulations of their administrator, the Sisters lost all of their property and had to abandon their charitable endeavors. Mother Clelia was deserted by everyone except twelve of her former daughters. Her courage never left her, however. Neither did her trust in Divine Providence. She was anxious and ready to begin anew. But no bishop could be found with enough confidence in her ability, and no benefactor came forward to offer aid and encouragement. In this heartbreaking situation someone suggested to Mother Clelia that she seek the advice and the help of the saintly bishop of Piacenza. In the year 1900, after much prayer, Mother Clelia decided to go to him. Bishop Scalabrini received her and her companions with his usual graciousness and hospitality. He listened with profound attention to her account of the terrible trials she and her Sisters had undergone. Then the Servant of God, as though inspired, made up his mind to take the new foundation under his protection. He encouraged the small group and assured them that if they were willing to dedicate themselves to the assistance of Italian immigrants, he would from that very moment consider himself their father and their protector.

He gave the Sisters temporary quarters in a country house and re-established the novitiate. He revised the rules which had been previously compiled by Mother Clelia and had them printed bearing his approval. He also made several changes in the religious habit of the Sisters, changes which gave it its present appearance. In the same year he was also able to acquire a beautiful and spacious residence in Piacenza. There he established the mother house of the order.

Vocations soon became numerous, and in a comparatively short time Bishop Scalabrini had the great joy of giving the crucifix to several groups of missionary Sisters departing for North and South America.

The servant of God continued to take a paternal interest in all the affairs of the new congregation until his unexpected death halted his efforts. But he had infused renewed life and a strong apostolic spirit into the new order. The tender plant grew to a giant tree whose branches extend today from Italy to the two Americas and to Asia Minor. It has more than 2,000 members.

These various religious organizations founded or directed toward the assistance of the immigrants by Bishop Scalabrini will remain as a living testimonial to his burning zeal, his organizing genius, and will ever be faithful to his ideal.

CHAPTER 30

Twilight and Sunset

. . . the call from the
Great Beyond . . .

Bishop Scalabrini could have been called an "outstanding bishop" even had he not made his own the holy cause of the Italian emigrants. However, the stupendous work he did and the success he achieved along this line elevate him so high above many of his colleagues that the question as to why he was never raised to the purple is both a natural and a logical one. For so zealous a bishop, so deserving in view of all he had done, the red hat should have represented the just recognition of his work. Why, then, was he never made a cardinal?

There are several reasons for this, and to many these may be considered unsatisfactory. Chief among them is the bishop's own humility, his own sense of unworthiness.

In 1901, when the date of his episcopal jubilee was rapidly approaching, he was making a retreat. He wrote to Pope Leo XIII, asking for a father's blessing, "one of those blessings which revive, comfort, and force the soul to rise above itself and its innate imperfections."

In this same letter we read: "If I look upon what I have done, in the midst of great difficulties, I find the means for rejoicing in the Lord. But if I delve deep into the inner recesses of my spirit, I find there only the material for regret for all I have neglected to do or have done so imperfectly. Of one thing, Beloved Father, I can assure you, and that is that I have no other goal than the glory of God and the salvation of the souls of men who have been entrusted to my care. The short span of life which God may yet grant me I now intend to consecrate entirely to the Church, that her cause may be advanced, that her sacrosanct, divine rights may be safe-guarded, and that I may draw my flock ever closer and closer to Your August Person."

Several years before, when in private audience with Leo XIII, the latter had hinted at raising him to the purple. It was at the time of the struggle between the Transigents and the Intransigents. The bishop had refused the honor. The thought of any honors being conferred upon his person, while some of his ideas were being condemned, was repugnant to him.

Later he refused the offer of an appointment as apostolic delegate to the United States. In 1901 the Italian press began to circulate the rumor that the bishop of Piacenza was to be elevated to the archdiocese of Ravenna. As arch-bishop of that city, he would almost automatically be raised to the purple. At the first confidential news he received of this the bishop hastened to write, begging that the nomina-tion be turned to other channels, and that the plan be si-lenced and forgotten.

Why this obstinate refusal of honors which are the natural steps in the career of a bishop who has become known for his spiritual qualities as well as for his gifts of leadership? We learn the answer from his own pen. No sooner had Bishop Bonomelli heard the news that his good friend was to be sent to Ravenna as archbishop than he hastened to write to him of his great happiness and satisfaction. His own wish would have been to see his friend not only an arch-bishop, but also a cardinal. This would have pleased him even more.

"Accept, I beg of you . . . make the great sacrifice," he wrote.

Bishop Scalabrini answered immediately:

"I cannot hide anything from you as to what is going on.

A little over two weeks ago a distinguished personality wrote me these words among others: 'Your Excellency will be nominated archbishop of Ravenna. What do you think of it?' I answered: 'I feel it is impossible for me to accept and if Your Excellency can help me in any way if the need should arise, I shall be most grateful to you.' For me to change dioceses now when I am so advanced in years is out of the question. Just now while my devoted clergy is preparing so diligently along with my flock to honor my coming jubilee it is impossible. To live, to sanctify myself (and it is about time), and to die in my Piacenza . . . this is what I have resolved to do each year during the spiritual exercises. God always accepts such prayers and promises. I beg of you, therefore, to keep this in absolute secrecy, for the plan you have in mind will not succeed. As far as I am concerned, I do not even speak of it with my faithful secretary who has been my constant companion for twenty-five years and who has shared my few joys and my many sorrows."

But what the Servant of God kept from his friend we also find openly expressed in his diary:

". . . to reject immediately any ambitious idea for a change of status, to rejoice at another's elevation, to ponder upon gaining God's favor in the position I now occupy, wherein I must sanctify myself and make my preparation for a good death. . . ."

And again:

". . . to sanctify myself as bishop of Piacenza . . . the rest is non-existent . . ."

In the last analysis, then, Bishop Scalabrini may be said to have fled from the purple from a spirit of true humility, springing forth from that very low concept in which he held himself and which often led him to refer to himself as "a poor sinner most unworthy of being a member of the episcopate."

For the sake of the virtue of humility, yes, but also for the sake of love—love of his flock. His people loved him and venerated him, each and all. He imposed himself upon them with the spirit of "true authority," that is the authority that is born of good well done, but he loved them also with the love of a father and a shepherd.

Each morning—and for so many years—as soon as he had arisen and dressed, no matter how fine or how inclement the weather, he opened wide his window and standing there he imparted an all-enfolding blessing upon his city and his diocese. The gesture was full of that gentle quality of a loving father who for the sake of his children watches over them even as they sleep. He offered them the early-morning gift of a prayer for their well-being. For the sake of these people he wanted to stay in Piacenza, he could not leave them though leaving might mean occupying a seat in the Sacred College.

The people of Piacenza learned of this somehow. They felt proud and yet humble in their appreciation of the devoted affection of a man so universally admired not only throughout Italy but also beyond its boundaries.

In the three years between his return from the United States and his departure for South America Bishop Scalabrini did not know the meaning of the word "rest." His pastorals—the last—reach up toward the Eternal with increasing strength and inspiration. The very subjects, "Devotion to the Blessed Sacrament," "The Sanctification of the Sabbath Day," "The Excellency of Prayer," manifest the need in his heart for an absolute union with his Maker.

No one thought that not too long a period of time would pass before he would leave this earth to continue his prayers where prayers for those we love will be made perfect.

As has been hinted before, Bishop Scalabrini had been suffering for some years from a physical discomfort about which he had spoken to no one, not having considered it serious. In Brazil the long rides on horseback had increased

the discomfort and he had mentioned it to his faithful servant, but only as a cross to be borne. On his return to Italy
he began to realize that the state of his health was not good.

Once again people broached the subject of his elevation
to the sacred purple to him, a fact which at the time was no
longer a mystery. Well aware that his health was on the de-
cline, his answer seemed stereotyped:

"I am old and I must turn my thoughts to my departure
from this earth."

And indeed he did. Every day half of his meditation time
was spent on this subject. However, he had no idea that his
death was actually as near as it was. Thus, almost as an un-
conscious premonition of it, he decided to reorganize his
diocese along more definite lines and to place his work for
the emigrants on more solid foundations.

Accustomed as he was to carry out any decision he might
make as soon as possible, on May 5, 1905, he announced his
sixth pastoral visit. The opening lines of his letter to his people state: "I have decided personally to conduct another
visit to all my parishes in the diocese." It was to be initiated on June 11, the Feast of Pentecost.

In this letter, short though it was, we find a thread of restrained melancholy. Between the lines transpire the
thoughts which had by now become habitual to him, and
there breathes in every word the loftiness which his love for
his flock had reached.

"Thirty years have passed since this outstanding portion
of Christ's flock has been entrusted to my care," he writes.
"Someday which I feel is not too far off I shall have to give a
strict account of my work to my Maker. Shall I then be able
to say to him with a serene countenance, 'Lord, the people
Thou gavest me I have nurtured and none of them has been
lost through my own fault'? This is a frightening thought
and it is ever before me. It harasses me, it urges me on to
make reparation for the failings and the mistakes of my

lengthy episcopate and leads me to undertake another general and purposeful pastoral visit.

"If I were to ponder on my age, I should naturally be perturbed, but my desire to see you all once more and to talk to you as your shepherd and your father is so profound that any difficulty is as nothing, any hardship light. In the name of God, therefore, I shall come to you. How satisfied I shall be indeed, if at the close of my visit I shall be able to say with the Apostle, 'I have been all to all, that I might win all souls unto Christ.' To win all to Christ is the supreme aspiration of my life and of my soul."

He begged his priests to co-operate with him especially with their prayers and to work zealously that their parishes might be in perfect order, laying particular emphasis on what concerned the cult and devotion due to the Holy Eucharist. It is evident from these words that as he felt himself near to the time when his God would reveal himself to him in all of his glory he experienced a more urgent need of drawing closer to His veiled Presence in the Sacrament of His love.

In the same letter Bishop Scalabrini also gave notice of having prepared a long "Questionnaire" which was to be sent to all the pastors in the diocese. They were to have a year's time in which to answer all the questions. Their successors would then be able to understand from these answers exactly what was the moral and material status of each parish in the early years of the twentieth century.

If Bishop Scalabrini had been able to carry out these intentions and again see his people, he would have received spectacular manifestations of their devotion toward him. He himself, in his humility and conscientious attitude toward his work, felt there was as yet much to do in this world. But God judged his work as a *fait accompli*. The time had come to call his faithful servant home to receive his well-earned reward.

On May 21 the bishop was officiating at the blessing of a

new cemetery. Toward the end of the ceremony he was suddenly taken ill. It was only a momentary thing, but he felt it was a warning. On the way home to his residence a funeral procession met him on the road. He asked that his carriage be halted, that he might step out and bless the remains.

"Soon, dear son, you will be reciting the prayers for the dead for me also," he said to his companion, Monsignor Mondini, as he finished.

What he said came true. A few days later he was taken ill again, and then, suddenly, his condition took a turn for the worse.

His relatives were notified and they hastened to his side. Two doctors confirmed the necessity of an immediate operation. The bishop was reluctant at first, but on their insistence he submitted himself to the ordeal.

The operation was performed on May 28. It lasted a half hour and was pronounced successful. All of that Sunday and part of the following Monday everything seemed satisfactory. Toward evening the patient's condition worsened. The next day his heart took on new strength and a ray of hope filled the hearts of the anxious watchers.

Hope faded again that night when his heart became weaker and weaker as the hours passed. That great heart which had beat so steadfast and strong whenever sorrowing souls had to be comforted and heavy burdens made lighter was losing its grip on life.

On Wednesday evening the bishop received the Last Sacraments and asked that they be given to him in solemn form. The bells of the cathedral were heard as the ceremony proceeded. Bishop Scalabrini asked for his surplice and pectoral cross and himself intoned the prayers while the sacrament of Extreme Unction was administered to him.

"I am about to appear before my Lord," he said as they were concluded. "I forgive all and give them my blessing. Pray for me . . . remember me to everyone . . . good-by . . ."

The long ceremony had exhausted him, and he fell asleep. When his doctor was questioned as to the possibility of saving his patient's life, he answered:

"Humanly, it is impossible."

Now and again during the night the bishop awoke. He was fully conscious, and on being notified that the Pope had sent his special blessing, he was deeply moved.

"Give him the grateful thanks of a son," were among his last words.

As soon as the seriousness of the bishop's illness had become known in his diocese, a never-ending prayer rose to the throne of the Almighty that his life be spared. People of all classes came to inquire of his condition. His great friend, Bishop Bonomelli, longed to be near him, but the celebration of his episcopal jubilee demanded his presence in Cremona.

"This was to be a day of great rejoicing for me," he said, "but it has become a day of the deepest sorrow."

Everyone in Italy—and indeed many beyond its frontiers—prayed for the bishop.

But the immense chorus of prayers did not succeed in obtaining the longed-for petition. The Voice that was calling the shepherd home to participate in the joy of the Lord had pronounced its irrevocable sentence.

At six o'clock, on the morning of June 1, his pale lips opened slightly. The invocation, "Jesus, the Way, the Truth, and the Life," came in a low whisper. His lips were sealed for eternity, lips that had never opened except to pray, teach, bless, comfort, or pity.

It was the day of the Ascension of Our Lord. The soul of Bishop Scalabrini who, like Christ, had loved all on earth, suffered, struggled, and won through the power of charity, that soul ascended to the higher spheres, into the dwellings where love ever renews itself in God!

CHAPTER 31

"The Just Shall Flourish
Like the Palm-tree"

*. . . the work must go on
and does . . .*

AFTER THE DEATH of Bishop Scalabrini there were those
who feared that the Pious Society of the Missionaries
of St. Charles, whose work had been so close to his heart,
was destined for an imminent end. But according to the Gospel, the works of the righteous flourish, even after they have
left this earth, for their work is willed and blessed by God.
In fact His Holiness St. Pius X assured the new superior
general of the society, Father Dominic Vicentini, that he
himself would support the efforts of the society with his
fatherly care. He added that this would be in homage to the
great bishop of Piacenza who was so well loved by him, and
also because the work done by the society was truly useful,
noble, and holy.

Thus, due to the kindly interest of St. Pius X, and in later
years of Benedict XV, Pius XI, and Pius XII, the Scalabrinian Fathers not only withstood all of the storms in their path,
but became strong, grew and developed to such an extent
that today they shed their beneficent influence upon practically every nation where there are Italian immigrants in any
considerable number.

In this chapter we shall limit ourselves to give just a mere
outline of the splendid developments achieved by these missionaries.

The main thought in the mind of Bishop Scalabrini's successor was the strengthening of the groundwork of the society. The urgency of the need for spiritual assistance to the immigrants had made clear to Bishop Scalabrini the necessity of recruiting his missionaries mainly from among the diocesan clergy. However, after his death, in order to assure to the society its peculiar permanent nature, it was found necessary to give life to regular training schools dedicated to the nurturing of missionary vocations. With this in view, Father Vicentini transferred the general mother house to Rome, and initiated the construction of a new minor seminary in the diocese of Treviso.

This training work, however, was brusquely interrupted by the outbreak of World War I. All of the priests and seminarians who were eligible were drafted into the army and the flow of vocations was halted almost completely. This made it impossible for the superior general to find young recruits to replace the missionaries who had grown old or who had passed on to their just reward. This situation lasted many years and forced the Scalabrinians to give up many a parish to other groups. In the United States alone thirty parishes met this fate, and yet each of them had been founded by the Scalabrinians among the Italians.

As soon as the war ended, Italian immigration took a tremendous leap. The United States opened its doors to almost a half million Italians between 1920 and 1930. To keep pace with this, the Missionaries of St. Charles recruited many new priests and many new aspirants into the ranks of those who devoted themselves to missionary work.

An economic depression followed the illusory prosperity of the post-war years. Old racial and nationalistic prejudices once again came to the fore. Almost every country was led to pass restrictive measures against immigration. The United States started this trend. In 1924 it approved a law which drastically reduced the total number of immigrants

to be admitted annually. It was limited to 150,000. The
United States also introduced the discriminatory formula
of the National Origins Quota System, which provided for
the distribution of immigration permits to the different
nationalities. On the basis of this formula, Italy was permitted a mere 5,000 visas annually. This was utterly insufficient. It could not even allow for the reunion of families who had been separated by previous emigrations and
who were expecting to be complete again.

This halt in European emigration in general and in Italian emigration in particular could be only temporary. All
immigration experts foresaw the fact that once political and
economic situations returned to normal, millions of Italians
would no doubt once again turn their faces westward. But
this time, contrary to what had occurred at the time of the
great emigration wave, the Church realized that she had to
be ready to meet the situation with her care of the immigrants.

Hence, the Sacred Consistorial Congregation—under
which His Holiness, Pius XI, in fulfillment of the plan presented by Bishop Scalabrini to St. Pius X, had placed the
Society of St. Charles since 1923—continued to further its
development. It was under the direction of the Sacred Consistorial Congregation that the order opend four new seminaries and one novitiate in Italy.

Worthy of note are the following:

1. The Scalabrinian Seminary, an imposing modern building, capable of housing more than 300 seminarians, rises
proudly and strong at the foot of the Venetian Alps. It was
built in 1930 in commemoration of the twenty-fifth anniversary of Bishop Scalabrini's death.

2. The Scalabrini-O'Brien Seminary, built near Bishop
Scalabrini's native town through the generosity of Archbishop William D. O'Brien, Auxiliary Archbishop of Chicago
and president of the Catholic Church Extension Society.

3. The St. Charles International College in Rome, for the seminarians destined for university studies.

In the meantime, the process of assimilation going on among the second generation of Italian immigrants made possible and opportune the fulfillment of another of Bishop Scalabrini's dreams. This was the hope of opening seminaries in countries where Italian immigrants were present. As early as February 8, 1891, in Rome, lecturing on emigration before an exceptionally large audience, he said: "I hope to realize the long-cherished dream of establishing a seminary for the children of Italian immigrants who may feel the calling to the priesthood and the generous impulse of the apostolate." These seminaries were to train priests among the sons of immigrants. Bishop Scalabrini thought, and justly so, that these young men, born within the bosom of two interlocked cultural backgrounds, that of the family that had come from Italy and that of the new society at large, would have a much wider opportunity of understanding the social and religious problems concerning the immigrants. Thus they would be in a much better position for tackling and solving such problems. After all, had not these young men through personal experience learned of the conflicts that the integration of two cultures brings? Did they not possess the positive elements of both these cultures? Were not most of them able to speak both languages? Bearing this idea of his great predecessor both in mind and heart, the superior of the order opened a novitiate in the United States during the second half of the 1940's, with a major and a minor seminary for English-speaking candidates. He did the same in Brazil for countries where Spanish and Portuguese were the mother tongues.

During this same period the Sacred Congregation encouraged the Scalabrinian Fathers to open missionary centers in France, Belgium, Luxembourg, and Argentina.

World War II broke out about this time. On the heels of the signing of an agreement between the Italian and the German governments tens of thousands of Italian working-men were transferred to Germany to replace the Germans who had been recruited into the army from the fields and the factories. The Sacred Consistorial Congregation sent a notable number of Scalabrinian Fathers to assist this army of Italian workers. They shared with them the hardships and the heartbreaks of wartime living, and after the Russian occupation, the concentration camps.

After World War II, Italy found herself with a depleted treasury, destroyed industries, a shattered economic status, and 3,000,000 unemployed. Almost as many were working at starvation wages. Added to these unfortunates were the refugees from Venetia Giulia and from the former African colonies. It was only natural that under such conditions the Italians who still nurtured some hope and energy to rebuild their broken lives for the future looked forward to leaving Italy for other shores. For them it was their only chance of salvation. And so began the new trek away from the native land.

Obstacles arose against this legitimate aspiration, this natural right of man, obstacles raised by the new immigration laws in the different countries where the immigrants wished to go. But in spite of these obstacles more than one and a half million Italians went to other countries of Europe, to North and South America, and to Australia between 1946 and 1953.

More often than not the laws on immigration are not based on authentic principles, whether economic or political, but on fears and prejudices, both irrational and egotistical, but they do exist and have to be faced. This emigration will have to go on for at least another ten years. There are some 2,000,000 more Italians who must find work and bread elsewhere than in Italy, so that those who will remain in that land may reach a decent standard of living for themselves, and a door to a better future.

In order to be of real assistance to present and future emigrants, the Scalabrinians are today building a network of parishes and missionary centers where this need is or will be felt.

As to the nature of their apostolate, these missionaries are not limited to one particular method. They adapt themselves in their activities to the special situations and to the specific needs of the immigrants in any given region. Where these immigrants have become a permanent entity and are present in considerable numbers that are enough to support a parish, the missionaries immediately set about organizing an Italian parish with all the necessary parochial activities within the parish. Where the immigrants are not stable or live in small groups far away from one another, the Scalabrinian Fathers establish missionary centers from which their activities radiate out into the surrounding country. Every type of activity, whether of educational value or strictly in the field of assistance, forms part of their aim and goal. Work which is of a definite parochial nature and is subsidiary to that which is already in existence in local parishes is today governed throughout the world by exact canonical regulations, as written in the Apostolic Constitution *Exul Familia*.

In France, in addition to a parish right in the center of Paris and an old people's home, the missionaries of Bishop Scalabrini care for nine missionary centers located in regions where the Italians have settled. In Switzerland, besides an orphanage and an old people's home in Geneva, they maintain five missionary centers, located in the principal cities. In Luxembourg and in Belgium they give of their aid and advice to the miners and the laborers of the region, reaching out from five more centers. In Argentina the apostolate among the Italians heads a group of six parishes and three missionary centers.

The missionaries cover the surrounding region with what are known as the "flying missions." These missions are held weekly from October through June. If the immigrants live in the territory covered by a particular parish, the missionary makes the proper arrangements with the local pastor. Then in a week spent in steadfast labors he visits all of the Italian families, inviting them to attend a three-day mission to be given in the parish church or at some other designated place. These missions aim at keeping the Catholic faith alive among the immigrants, at regulating marriages, seeing to it that every child born within the past year has been baptized, and giving everyone a chance and an opportunity of making his annual confession and receiving Holy Communion. These missions also serve to bind closer the relationship between the immigrants and the local pastors. Through the missionaries the immigrants can obtain the right approach, an approach which the immigrant would seldom dare to make of his own initiative.

The flying missions are only one of the means used by the Scalabrinians in their missionary activity. They also make use of the radio and the press. Almost every missionary center publishes a monthly bulletin and in France and Switzerland a weekly is published, called the *Eco.* The *Eco* is for the special use of the immigrants living in those countries.

During these years the old missions in Brazil and in the United States have continued to progress and to build new churches, schools, and recreational centers, thus fulfilling the need of the moment.

More parishes have been added to the thirty-one already flourishing in Brazil. Mention should be made of a great center built in São Paulo, next to the imposing and very modern Church of Our Lady of Peace. In Rio Grande do Sul the Fathers operate a radio station besides their other activities.

In the United States there is hardly one among the thirty-seven parishes cared for by the Scalabrinians which has not undergone great changes for the better. Practically all of their churches breathe the warmth of sacred Italian art and at the same time are not without modern conveniences. Modern parochial schools rise near the churches.

Among the most noteworthy churches are those of Everett, Massachusetts, and Thornton, Rhode Island, which rank high even in comparison with the most artistic and beautiful of New England. Villa Scalabrini, the rest home for old Italians in Chicago, is one of the finest in the United States. Samuel Cardinal Stritch said of it:

"A monument raised by the Scalabrinian Fathers to the tenacity of the Catholic Italian immigrants, who have contributed so much to the diffusion of the Catholic religion in this archdiocese and to its consolidation."

A vivid proof of the strength and growth of the Scalabrinian missions in the United States is the fact that not only have they become self-supporting, but they have opened new missions outside of the States: one in Canada and sixteen in Australia. The Most Reverend James H. Griffiths, auxiliary bishop of the United States Armed Forces, speaking of the Scalabrinians, explained in glowing terms the significance of this new growth on the occasion of the departure of a group of Scalabrinian missionaries for Australia.

"Fifty years ago the servant of God, Bishop Scalabrini, sent his first missionaries to the United States to preserve the Faith among the Italian immigrants. Today the Scalabrinian missionaries gather in the fruits of their labors. They behold the sons of those immigrants of old being educated and inspired to become priests, thus becoming 'emigrants' once again, not to seek a loaf of bread which their native land cannot offer, but to carry the comfort of the Faith to those who, as once did their own parents, must bid adieu to their beloved villages or towns that they may build for a better life on a foreign soil. This is a living proof that the Italian colony in the United States has reached man's stature, in the Faith as well as in all other sectors of human endeavor. And this is no small merit of Bishop Scalabrini, who at this moment from his place in heaven must be exulting in this inspiring sight, the sight of a continuous renewal of the finest missionary tradition of Italian Catholics."

In August of 1952 His Holiness Pius XII promulgated the Apostolic Constitution on the Spiritual Care of the Emigrants, *Exul Familia*. This crowned the dream Bishop Scalabrini had dreamed for so many years. In 1905, shortly before his death, Bishop Scalabrini had given St. Pius X his plan for the reorganization of all the agencies which were of aid and assistance to the emigrants. They had to be subjected to the jurisdiction of the Sacred Consistorial Congregation. He had submitted his plan for a systematic codification of all the laws and regulations issued through the years with regard to the care of the immigrants.

In the *Exul Familia* the Holy Father vindicates the right of the Church as well as her duty to assist the emigrants spiritually as part of the universal mandate to save souls, a mandate enjoined on her by Christ. He stresses the need and importance of a spiritual assistance adapted to the special conditions of the emigrants. Pointing out that such an assistance can be adequately rendered only by priests who know the language, the background, the culture of the emigrants, the Pontiff promulgates laws regulating this special apostolate. Thus, today, the work among the immigrants is governed the world over by the exact canonical rules set forth in the "Apostolic Constitution," *Exul Familia*, which stands as the Magna Carta of the Church on emigration.

In the momentous "act" the Holy Father, recalling the documented history of the care offered to the emigrants throughout the centuries by the Church, summarizes also the history of the Pious Society of the Missionaries of St. Charles, concluding thus:

"The present development of the Scalabrinian Fathers gives rise to the highest hopes for a more secure and stable spiritual assistance of the Italian emigrants in the future."

Since we have wished to treat of the "Life and Works of Bishop Scalabrini," it is only natural that we are focusing our attention on the apostolate as carried on by the Scalabrinian Fathers. But this must not lead anyone to think even for a moment that they have been the only priests from Italy or of Italian extraction who took an interest in the work dedicated to the interest of the Italian immigrants. Most numerous indeed have been the priests, whether secular or religious, who were and are dedicated to the tilling of the soil and then to the nurturing of the tender plants with their unstinting efforts, the same soil and the same plants over which the Scalabrinians have labored and are laboring today.

They too are "Pioneers and Apostles" worthy of the deepest gratitude of the millions of emigrants whose roots were watered and fed by the teaching of the Catholic Church under the beneficent rays of the Italian sun.

PRAYER TO THE BLESSED TRINITY
FOR THE
GLORIFICATION OF THE SERVANT OF GOD

✠

O Blessed Trinity, Who sanctify and glorify souls, we ardently beseech Thee that for Thine honor and for the honor of the Church, Thou wilt make resplendent the merits of Thy servant, John Baptist Scalabrini.

His life was always filled with a living Faith, which he, with illumined zeal, awakened in his sons and wanted preserved in the emigrants, through the work of his Missionaries; with a firm Hope, which he always kept undimmed in his trials and sufferings; and with an ardent Charity, which he diffused zealously in his apostolic ministry for Thine honor, for the honor of the Blessed Virgin and of the Saints, and for the alleviation of his fellowmen.

Relying on these merits, O Lord, we are confident that Thou hast crowned his soul with eternal joy; but we beseech Thee that also here on earth he may be honored with the aureole of sanctity. Amen.

✠

Those who obtain favors through the intercession of the Servant of God, Bishop Scalabrini, are asked to notify the Superior of:

ST. CHARLES SEMINARY, STATEN ISLAND 4, N. Y.

or

SACRED HEART SEMINARY, MELROSE PARK, ILL.

✠

With Ecclesiastical Approbation

241

PRESENT SCALABRINIAN PARISHES
IN THE UNITED STATES AND CANADA

Blessed Virgin of Pompei, Milwaukee, Wis.
Holy Cross, Providence, R. I.
Holy Ghost, Providence, R. I.
Holy Guardian Angel, Chicago, Ill.
Immaculate Conception, Eveleth, Minn.
Our Lady of All Souls, Hamilton, Ontario, Canada
Our Lady of Loreto, East Providence, R. I.
Our Lady of Mount Carmel, Bristol, R. I.
Our Lady of Mount Carmel, Melrose Park, Ill.
Our Lady of the Holy Rosary, Kansas City, Mo.
Our Lady of Pompei, Chicago, Ill.
Our Lady of Pompei, New York, N. Y.
Sacred Heart, Boston, Mass.
Sacred Heart, Cincinnati, O.
St. Anthony, Buffalo, N. Y.
St. Anthony, Chicago, Ill.
St. Anthony, Everett, Mass.
St. Anthony, Fredonia, N. Y.
St. Anthony, New Haven, Conn.
St. Anthony, Somerville, Mass.
St. Bartholomew, Providence, R. I.
St. Callistus, Chicago, Ill.
St. Charles Borromeo, Melrose Park, Ill.
St. Frances Xavier Cabrini, Chicago, Ill.
St. Joachim, New York, N. Y.
St. John the Baptist, Kansas City, Mo.
St. Joseph, New York, N. Y.
St. Lazarus, East Boston, Mass.
St. Lucy's Mission, Chicago, Ill.
St. Maria Addolorata, Chicago, Ill.
St. Maria Incoronata, Chicago, Ill.
St. Mary of Mount Carmel, Utica, N. Y.
St. Michael, Chicago, Ill.
St. Michael, New Haven, Conn.
St. Peter, Syracuse, N. Y.
St. Rita, Milwaukee, Wis.
St. Rocco, Thornton, R. I.
St. Tarcisius, Framingham, Mass.
Villa Scalabrini, North Lake City (Melrose Park), Ill.

FORMER SCALABRINIAN PARISHES
IN THE UNITED STATES AND CANADA

Christ the King, Daphne, Ala.
Hammonton Mission, Hammonton, N. J.
Immaculate Conception, Iron Mountain, Mich.
Most Precious Blood, New York, N. Y.
Our Lady Help of Christians, St. Louis, Mo.
Our Lady of Graces, Johnston, R. I.
Our Lady of Mount Carmel, Cincinnati, O.
Our Lady of Mount Carmel, Cortlandt, N. Y.
Our Lady of Mount Carmel, Meriden, Conn.
Our Lady of Mount Carmel, Providence, R. I.
Our Lady of Pompei, Monangah, W. Va.
Our Lady of Pompei, Syracuse, N. Y.
Our Lady of the Holy Rosary, Bridgeport, Conn.
Our Lady of the Holy Rosary, Chicago, Ill.
Our Lady of the Holy Rosary, Cleveland, O.
Our Lady of the Holy Rosary, Jersey City, N. J.
Our Lady of the Holy Rosary, Winnipeg, Canada
Sacred Heart, New Haven, Conn.
Sacred Heart Orphanage, Kearny, N. J.
St. Ambrose, St. Louis, Mo.
St. Ann, Hamden, Conn.
St. Ann, Providence, R. I.
St. Anthony, Cincinnati, O.
St. Anthony, Joliet, Ill.
St. Bartholomew, Norwich, N. Y.
St. Charles, St. Louis, Mo.
St. Francis, Detroit, Mich.
St. Francis' Chapel, New Orleans, La.
St. John the Baptist, Columbus, O.
St. Joseph, Fairmont, W. Va.
St. Joseph, Tontitown, Ark.
St. Louis, Oswego, N. Y.
St. Lucy, Newark, N. J.
St. Mary, New Orleans, La.
St. Paul, Erie, Pa.
St. Peter the Apostle, Pittsburgh, Pa.

Index

245